DEFINING
INDIA

DEFINING
INDIA

Through Their Eyes

SONIA SINGH

PENGUIN
VIKING
An imprint of Penguin Random House

VIKING

USA | Canada | UK | Ireland | Australia
New Zealand | India | South Africa | China | Singapore

Viking is part of the Penguin Random House group of companies
whose addresses can be found at global.penguinrandomhouse.com

Published by Penguin Random House India Pvt. Ltd
4th Floor, Capital Tower 1, MG Road,
Gurugram 122 002, Haryana, India

Penguin
Random House
India

First published in Viking by Penguin Random House India 2019

10 9 8 7 6 5 4 3 2

ISBN 9780670091935

Typeset in Adobe Garamond Pro by Manipal Digital Systems, Manipal
Printed at Replika Press Pvt. Ltd, India

www.penguin.co.in

This is a legitimate digitally printed version of the book and therefore might not
have certain extra finishing on the cover.

This book is dedicated to my mother Amrita Varma. Mummy, this one is for you.

Also in memory of my late grandfather Brigadier Shanti Saroop Malik. I hope he would have enjoyed reading this.

To my husband, R.P.N. Singh. Thank you for believing I could do this.

And to our girls, Suhaani, Raagini, Yaamini—just know, everything I do, I do it for you.

Contents

Preface

This book began because of a deep and abiding curiosity about the many Indias that over a billion people live in. Yet, there are some moments that transcend all divides to leave a lasting impact on the psyche of one nation.

What are the defining moments in India's history in the twenty-first century and why? What changes did they bring about and how did they impact India?

As an observer and reporter of the changes in India for the last twenty-seven years, I set out to speak to the men and women who have been integral participants in different moments of contemporary India—what they felt at the time, their unique perspective and, most importantly, what drives them. While all of these men and women are leaders in their field and are icons in their own right, I wanted to explore what young Indians can learn from these people who have made history in so many ways.

Over the last year, I've had a series of rare conversations with extraordinary Indians who kindly agreed to share their views from their vantage points in history with me—they include three Bharat Ratnas and three Nobel Laureates, among others.

Every conversation left me enriched and that to me is the essence of a good interview. To illuminate a thought, an idea, a moment in time.

For instance, I had interviewed Pranab Mukherjee a number of times when he was in the highest of government positions, have seen him in the majestic grandeur of Rashtrapati Bhavan, however when I met him for this book, what struck me was how his stature hadn't diminished away from the trappings of power; in fact in an unexpected twist, he even received the Bharat Ratna at this time. Even in 'retirement', he remained keenly alive to the current political situation and his strong belief that India will not see the dominance of any one political party. What however transfixed me was listening to him describe the details of a prime minister's assassination, being at that traumatic time with her son, the next prime minister of India and taking the crucial call to keep Indira Gandhi 'alive' till her son was sworn in, even though it meant stepping aside from his own political ambitions. I believe that it was her death that shaped the life of the future President of India.

Then from a man who was by Indira Gandhi's side during the Emergency to the man who went to jail for opposing it, I spoke to Arun Jaitley. Though he is often criticized for not having won an election, it is fascinating to hear him describe how he fought the election for the position of Delhi University Students Union president with a prime minister campaigning against him and the legendary Jayaprakash Narayan (popularly referred to as JP) giving a speech in his favour. His praise also of the 1991 economic reforms brought in by political rival Manmohan Singh and his support of a family member's inter-faith marriage, all revealing of the fact that our political leaders are often done a disservice when we believe they are bound only by the narrow rigidities of party positions.

Nirmala Sitharaman by contrast is more cautious when we speak, dignified, her steeliness of demeanour and character shines through in the conversation, both when we talk of India's air strikes into Pakistan and the tragic aftermath of the killings of Indian paramilitary soldiers as well as the Rafale controversy. For her, being defence minister is not about being defined by her gender but about living up to a historic legacy, in which she cannot falter.

Amartya Sen, whom I met in Delhi, has visibly aged in the last few years, but intellectually stands as tall as ever. His choice of a defining moment for him personally goes back to when he was eleven years old and a man literally bled to death on his lap. He masterfully draws linkages to then and now and the common learnings from both.

I flew to Bangalore for my conversation with Nandan Nilekani, the man who shifted to Delhi's corridors of power for five years. He seemed much happier back home in Koramangala, the heart of start-up India, even as Aadhaar—the unique number which has literally touched all of our lives—piloted by him under the United Progressive Alliance (UPA) government was brought home by a prime minister who was once bitterly opposed to it. He talks of his 'persuasion' visits to then Gujarat chief minister and now Prime Minister Narendra Modi for Aadhaar and how he quickly became its biggest supporter. Own it, it's your scheme, he also told the Congress but realpolitik intervened.

Another brilliant mind of the UPA era, Raghuram Rajan who made the transition to work under the Modi government as well, talked extensively of the time he came to India, almost as a form of 'national service', when the rupee was in a downward spiral. More importantly, he tells me he expressed his opposition to demonetization 'at the highest levels of government'. He also speaks frankly of the criticism levelled against him for the whole bad-loan crisis pointing to the fact that on his watch, he couldn't just ignore it and let the problem get worse—he had to act despite the criticism that he shut down growth. Even in Chicago, he remains passionately engaged with the India story and its future.

And, of course, the superstars, both Aamir Khan and Kamal Haasan, spoke about taking on completely different roles from their film avatars—but there the similarity ends. Aamir Khan talks of the many different realities he lives in but is convinced he can change the world around him, doing what he does best, the art of communicating and public service but No Politics, please. Kamal Haasan has joined a world alien to him but as he tells me, he's been inspired by the 'greatest actor of them all', a man he looks up to for being 'imitable', Mahatma Gandhi.

I notice that unconsciously, completely different individuals often share similar traits. 'The Crusaders' is what I've called Kailash Satyarthi, Fali Nariman and Aruna Roy—all of them indefatigable and principled, determined to fight till the very end for causes they believe in: be it India's children, the right to information or the independence of the judiciary.

Kiran Mazumdar-Shaw and Sania Mirza spoke of how gender bias shaped their respective journeys and spurred them on, and how they tackled it doing what came naturally to them. Their stories are very different but as pioneers in their fields, they are role models for a whole younger generation today.

And of course, meeting the 'God of Cricket' was special. Sachin's calm dignity both on and off the field stands out at a time when aggression is cool. His incredible talent, humility and focus in pursuing a dream is worth emulating for today's cricketers.

Occupying a special place in my memories of writing this book is travelling to Dharamshala to speak to 'a Living God'—the Dalai Lama—a rare opportunity as his interactions and travel are now increasingly limited. In his McLeod Ganj residence, as we converse, he reveals a political bombshell (more on that in the book). It was a conscious decision to include him in this roll call of extraordinary Indians, as he says India is now his home. He has accepted that he will spend his last days on this soil as India's most famous refugee.

My endeavour has been to bring to you the human side of each of these people, the private person behind the very public persona we see only in headlines. I am grateful for the unprecedented access they gave me and the openness with which they spoke to me.

A special thanks to Meru who supported this idea wholeheartedly over cold coffee, the entire team at Penguin, Toonika, Premanka and Dipti, and, of course, my brilliant and very patient researchers, Parmeshwar Bawa and Yaamini Singh. I couldn't have done it without them. Much gratitude also to my mentors, Radhika and Prannoy Roy.

Suparna, thank you for being an eternal sounding board and most importantly, for all the pep talks. Debbie and Suhani, for being there through my idiosyncrasies and providing a break whenever needed. Heartfelt thanks also to my family, my brother Mohit, my uncles and aunts, Mohit, Jane, Peter, Anita and, of course, my mother-in-law, Mohini Devi, all of them avid readers.

None of this would have been possible without the constant love and support of my husband RPN, who has always had more faith in my abilities than I do and my wonderful mother, Amrita Varma, who has wholeheartedly backed me in all I wanted to do, whether it made sense or not, since I was a child.

And to my beautiful girls—Raagini, Suhaani and Yaamini—I hope you will be inspired by the ideas you read in this book.

[1]

Pranab Mukherjee

My Holy Book Is the Constitution;
My Temple, the Parliament of India

The country's newest Bharat Ratna recipient at eighty-three, Pranab Mukherjee, India's thirteenth President is now seen as India's most eminent statesman who is respected across party lines. Often referred to as the 'best prime minister India never had', his encyclopaedic knowledge of the Constitution has ensured that he is often the first port of call for consultations by both the previous and current prime minister. Pranab Mukherjee's heartfelt farewell speech as President rings true now more than ever before. He had said, 'For the past fifty years of my public life, my sacred book has been the Constitution of India, my temple has been the Parliament of India and my passion, the service of the People of India."

'That was a speech of sadness,' Pranab Mukherjee, seated behind a teak wood table in his book-lined study, tells me. 'When I look back, the one thing that strikes me is that the last fifty years of my life have revolved around these magnificent buildings of Parliament—this temple of democracy. When I first entered here on 13 July 1969—the day the monsoon session of Parliament began—I had no identity. Nobody knew me. All I had was a piece of paper—as a certificate of my election to the Rajya Sabha from West Bengal—given to me by the Secretary of the West Bengal Legislative Assembly. So, when I gave my final speech here, I looked at the audience sitting in front of me and it had members of Parliament [MPs], members of the Union Cabinet, state chief ministers, governors of states and representatives of the diplomatic corps from various countries. That day no one asked me, as the security people of the Rajya Sabha once did forty-eight years ago, "Who are you?"'

As a former President, Pranab Mukherjee has now stepped away from active political life but remains extremely relevant. In a political surprise, India's highest honour, the Bharat Ratna, was given to the lifetime Congressman by the Modi government, the announcement coming just a day before Republic Day in 2019.

'Prime Minister Modi called to ask for my acceptance at 6 p.m. on 25 January,' Pranab Mukherjee, tells me of the rare honour. 'He told me the normal practice is for him to come personally and take my consent, but he was busy with the visit of the South African president on the eve of Republic Day. However, the prime minister wanted the Bharat Ratna to be announced on that same evening, for Republic Day and he needed my assent before he could advise the President to issue the notification. "The President is waiting for my call with your approval," Mr Modi said to me. So, I gave my consent,' he says smiling as he recalls how he told no one till the announcement came from Rashtrapati Bhavan. 'My daughter, Sharmishta, who lives with me, was very angry with me. She said—"You are awarded the Bharat Ratna and you are behaving as if nothing has happened, you didn't even tell me." I said I was waiting for the formal notification. "What is a notification, why did you need to wait, surely if the prime minister of India calls you, there is no doubt," she shot back.' He laughs.

'What about the political messaging,' I ask, 'the fact that a BJP [Bharatiya Janata Party] prime minister chose you?'

'I feel this is a larger recognition, not a recognition of an individual,' he replies. 'In fact, in this case, I entirely agree with Rahul Gandhi. I felt this was one of the best tweets that ever came from him, when he tweeted shortly after the announcement— "Congratulations to Pranab da on being awarded the Bharat Ratna. The Congress takes great pride in the fact that the immense contribution to public service and nation building of one of our own, has been recognized and honoured." This is the recognition of one of *our* man's contribution,' Pranab Mukherjee says. 'That means a recognition of a Congressman's contribution. I take it in that way.'

A strong message of where his loyalties lie conveyed with the greatest subtlety by a political strategist who has often kept his own party guessing. 'So, you didn't find a certain irony in this?' I ask.

'No, not at all,' he replies. 'I also gave it to Atal Behari Vajpayee as President in May 2015. In fact, the Bharat Ratna is the only award in India which the President decides. All the other Padma Awards have an elaborate process of selecting candidates, volumes of names are gone through, then there is a home ministry committee to review these names and all kinds of clearances needed before a shortlist is made for the prime minister and the Cabinet to approve.

The Bharat Ratna is meant to be decided by the President, however when I was President, I had resolved to go by every advice of the Cabinet. So, when Mr Modi proposed to me that Mr Vajpayee should be given the Bharat Ratna in 2015, I said, I have no problem, but I also suggested that someone else too should be given the award, perhaps posthumously. It was then that the late Madan Mohan Malaviya's [freedom fighter, educationist, founder of Banaras Hindu University and the Hindu Mahasabha] name was also proposed, and I accepted.'

'In fact,' he continues, 'in 1977, when Morarji Desai became prime minister, he said all these government awards are bunkum, he was totally against it, so they were scrapped. In 1978 and 1979, there were no awards. Indira Gandhi returned as prime minister twelve days before 26 January 1980. I was a minister in her Cabinet and the leader of the Rajya Sabha. Indira Gandhi and I were sitting together in the Rajya Sabha when she told me, Pranab, I want to start the Padma Awards again. I said there is no time to shortlist names for the Padma Awards before Republic Day, we can however choose a Bharat Ratna but it must be a person who is most distinguished. We discussed some names, then finally I said, why not Mother Theresa? Indira Gandhi jumped at it, saying, "What a good idea", but I cautioned her. We had to find out whether Mother Teresa was still an Albanian citizen or an Indian citizen because the Bharat Ratna can't go to a foreigner. When I checked, the officials told me, Sir, she is an Indian citizen, her name is being considered for the Padma Award. I laughed and said, forget the Padma Awards, she is getting the highest award of India. It was a choice that was welcomed across the board,' Pranab Mukherjee recalls. 'Only one award was given in 1980 but then the whole process started again.'

From choosing Bharat Ratnas to awarding them and now receiving one in his own right, life has come full circle for Pranab Mukherjee, a reflection of his eclectic political journey.

Once an unknown first-time MP plucked out of political obscurity by Indira Gandhi in 1969, he went on to become a key player in India's political narrative for the next five decades. Pranab Mukherjee has witnessed first-hand the Indira Gandhi days, the Emergency, her dramatic election loss and then her triumphant return, Operation Blue Star, her assassination, and then Rajiv Gandhi's, his widow's rise to power, going on to become the most powerful minister in the UPA government and then becoming the President of India himself during the tenure of two very different prime ministers—Manmohan Singh and Narendra Modi.

'As a participant in virtually every important contemporary political event, you have seen unimaginable changes. What have been the key milestones for our nation?' I ask.

'Defining moments in the history of a great nation like India are much more difficult to elucidate because these are just small bubbles in the vast ocean of its continuity. There are so many events in the vast magnitude of the Indian nation, because in the concept of the European nation state, India cannot be called a nation,' he replies, in typical Pranab-da style, referring to a lesson in world history and philosophy in his answer. 'The concept of the nation state in Europe developed after the Treaty of Westphalia in 1648. It was a treaty signed by various European warring factions which ended the thirty-year war. There, the nation state was defined as a group of people occupying a particular territory, having a common language, a common religion and more often than not, identifying as a community.

'However, today, as I am speaking to you, we use 122 languages and 1800 dialects in different parts of the country. We belong to three major ethnic groups, Caucasians, Dravidians and Mongoloids—each separate group doesn't have just ten, fifteen or 100 people as part of it but people in the thousands and millions. In our everyday lives, we practise seven major religions and we are 1.32 billion people. So, how can we say India is a nation state?' he asks rhetorically.

'Philosophically, for 5000 years, we have said we don't have any enemies. *Sarve Bhavantu Sukhinah, Sarve Santu Nir-Aamayaah, Sarve Bhadraanni Pashyantu, Maa Kashcid-Dukha-Bhaag-Bhavet* [Let everyone be happy. Let everyone be well, mentally and physically]. In this inclusive approach, where is the scope of identifying an enemy?'

'That's a very interesting interpretation,' I point out, 'because we often seem to look for enemies within our own nation.'

Skirting my interjection deftly, he continues, 'Therefore, what I am trying to say is that in this vast canvas of Indian civilization and nationhood, it is very difficult to define any particular moment which has changed India.'

'However, since the birth of our nation, our democracy has faced many difficult moments, which we have surprisingly overcome without much damage. Our experiment with democracy itself was a defining moment. Our country had been partitioned on the basis of religion. On 14 August 1947, at the stroke of the midnight hour, about 8 crore people, who were citizens of India, became aliens. On the day of Independence, I was just a twelve-year-old boy. Even though Bengal was partitioned, the arrival of refugees and communal riots did not impact me greatly as I read about these things in newspapers. It happened beyond my vision or presence as I was living in a remote village,' he says.

'You are underplaying the importance of your role as a participant in key events,' I say. 'For instance, even today, the BJP will bring up the Emergency as a turning point in Indian political history. The Congress says we are in a similar situation of an undeclared Emergency today. You were a key minister and confidant of Indira Gandhi during those years—do you regret it?'

He chooses his words carefully. 'Emergency is noted in the context of certain misrules. Emergency, in generic terms, is a constitutional provision. Articles 352, 353, 354 to 356 are provisions that deal with an emergency situation. The impact of the declaration of Emergency by Parliament curbed the fundamental rights of the people to some extent. That was the adverse impact. Freedom was affected. So, when we talk of the Emergency, we refer particularly to the abuse of emergency powers that curb freedom. When the BJP says Indira Gandhi imposed Emergency in June 1975, they mean during the Emergency for thirteen months, there were a lot of curtailments of people's rights. People were placed under detention without trial. When the Congress talks of an Emergency-like situation today, they mean that without declaring Emergency, the rights of individuals are being curbed. But this is a political battle in which I do not want a part. In hindsight, yes, the Emergency could have been avoided, it would have been better if it could have been avoided. I leave it to the future historians and researchers to educate and enlighten Indians.' That's as far as he will be drawn into this matter, but more than forty years later, it's clear that it is a regret for him.

'However,' he muses, 'the greatest challenge I have lived through, which brought about an unprecedented crisis for our nation, was when a sitting prime minister, Indira Gandhi, was assassinated. India had never faced a situation like this before.'

At the time of her assassination, Pranab Mukherjee was Indira Gandhi's closest political adviser and the highest-ranking minister in government. Thirty-five years later, the events are still vivid for him today.

'On 31 October 1984, Rajiv Gandhi and I were onstage at a rally in Kanthi, West Bengal. I had just finished speaking when I received a cryptic message. "The prime minister has been assaulted. Return to Delhi immediately." Rajiv was giving his speech, so I passed him a note asking him to cut it short. He did so, and we immediately started planning our return to Delhi. My colleague, Ghani Khan Choudhury, had his Mercedes while we were travelling in Ambassadors. He suggested we take his car, since it would be faster.

'Rajiv sat in the front with the driver, while Ghani Khan Choudhury, Rajiv's personal security officer and I sat at the back. Except that first message, we had no further updates. Rajiv had the radio tuned to the BBC, then at one point he turned to me and said, "Pranab, the BBC is saying sixteen bullets have been fired into her." He then turned to his personal security officer sitting next to me and asked, "This gun you're carrying to protect me, how potent are the bullets?" The poor man was at a loss how to answer, then he said sheepishly, "Very powerful, sir!" I tried to keep his hopes up by pointing out that the BBC had also reported that I, along with Rajiv, had reached Delhi, while we were still on the highway. I told him if they're wrong about this, they could be wrong about that too. However, the sense of foreboding wouldn't go away, as we drove silently on,' Pranab recounts.

'At Kolkata airport, we boarded a special plane to Delhi. Rajiv went into the cockpit. When he emerged, all he said was, "She is dead."'

The plane was full of senior Congress leaders and Rajiv Gandhi's statement was met with shock. While her son kept his composure, Pranab Mukherjee remembers breaking down.

'I was shattered. I just kept crying and crying. Sheila Dikshit, who was on the same flight, had to give me three or four handkerchiefs as I wet each one with my tears,' he says.

Despite his grief, Pranab's first instinct was to take charge of the situation. His political mentor was dead and there were rumours that Pranab Mukherjee expected to be sworn in as the next prime minister instead of the relatively inexperienced Rajiv Gandhi, who was a first-time MP at the time.

'Complete canards,' he says dismissively. 'I was number two in government then and I realized immediately there must be no vacuum between the death of a prime minister and the swearing in of a new one.

'Our first two prime ministers, Nehru and later Shastri, passed away while in office [27 May 1964 and 11 January 1966 respectively].

In both instances, an interim government was formed with Gulzari Lal Nanda, the senior-most minister, as interim prime minister. Then, however, the two sitting prime ministers had died a natural death. This was not the case with Indira Gandhi. I asked Rajiv to take over as prime minister and that he had to be sworn in as soon as we landed,' he says emphatically.

And then perhaps the most chilling part, a decision by the ever-pragmatic Pranab. 'Indira Gandhi had to be kept officially alive till Rajiv Gandhi was sworn in. Her death could not be announced. That message was relayed,' he concludes tersely.

When they landed in Delhi, the chief of army staff, the Cabinet Secretary and others were waiting to meet Rajiv Gandhi at the airport. It was at the airport that the Cabinet Secretary Krishnaswamy Rao Sahib told Pranab Mukherjee that he should be sworn in as interim prime minister because he was the senior-most minister after Indira Gandhi.

'But I refused,' remembers Pranab. 'I told the Cabinet Secretary, we have had an informal meeting on the aircraft, Rajiv, I and other senior Congress leaders like then Bengal Governor, Uma Shankar Dikshit, we have decided Rajiv Gandhi should take over as the next prime minister. The Cabinet Secretary immediately ordered Rajiv Gandhi's security to be enhanced and preparations began immediately.'

In the interim, a grieving son drove immediately to the hospital with his relative and MP Arun Nehru. A distraught Sonia Gandhi and Congress senior leaders were waiting for them. Pranab Mukherjee also drove directly to the hospital to see Indira Gandhi's body. The scene at the All India Institute of Medical Sciences in New Delhi was chaotic, with crowds thronging outside. No official announcement of her death had yet been made, but news that the larger-than-life leader who had so comprehensively dominated India's political landscape was gone had spread rapidly. As Pranab Mukherjee observed the people outside his car window, he had only

one thought: 'What would be the repercussions of this assassination?'
It was unheard of in independent India that a leader was killed by the
very men meant to protect her.

'When I arrived at the hospital, P.C. Alexander, the prime
minister's private secretary, along with Arun Nehru, were
organizing everything. In my mind, I questioned, who were
they, now? P.C. Alexander had no official powers any more after
the prime minister's death. Arun Nehru, too, was just one of
the 550 members of Parliament the Congress had in the Lok Sabha
and Rajya Sabha,' he says. 'Yet they both were playing a major role.'

'I realized that it was Arun Nehru and the others who were
spreading the rumours,' continues Pranab Mukherjee. 'They told me
that Vice President R. Venkataraman should immediately swear in
Rajiv instead of waiting for President Zail Singh who was abroad to
return and administer the oath. "Will you jeopardize the legitimacy
of the process?" I shot back. In the Constitution, a vice president is
only meant to oversee the Rajya Sabha. Instead, they tried to imply
that President Giani Zail Singh may refuse to swear Rajiv Gandhi
and swear me in instead because he was Sikh. They were just trying
to create a rift between us.'

However, in his memoir, *Through the Corridors of Power*,
P.C. Alexander set the record straight. 'I quickly told Pranab
Mukherjee that everyone had agreed that Rajiv Gandhi should be
administered the oath of office as prime minister without going
in for an interim arrangement. Without any hesitation, Pranab
Mukherjee gave his assent to this suggestion,' Alexander writes.
'A group of individuals with malicious intent later spread a
canard that Pranab Mukherjee had staked his claim to be sworn
in as interim PM and had to be persuaded with great difficulty to
withdraw his claim. I should record here the true facts.'

Rajiv Gandhi was eventually sworn in that night by
President Giani Zail Singh along with a small group of four ministers,
including Pranab Mukherjee. Twelve hours after her death, the

vice president announced the news about Indira Gandhi and the swearing in of a new government simultaneously on Doordarshan.

'Mrs Gandhi had to be kept "alive" till the new prime minister took over,' Pranab Mukherjee tells me. 'It's like they say in Great Britain—"The King is Dead, Long Live the King."

'There can be no vacuum.'

'You think she didn't know the risk after Operation Blue Star?' Pranab Mukherjee asks me, still visibly moved after so many years. 'Indira Gandhi had once said to me, "Pranab, I know I will die for this country."'

It was a premonition that came tragically true. The smooth political transition, however, came at an unacceptably high human cost. Delhi burned in the days after Indira Gandhi's killing, over 2,500 Sikhs were killed in the aftermath. 'Why did that happen on your government's watch? Was it a failure?' I ask him.

'The army was deployed too late,' he replies tersely. 'The home minister had been informed of the situation. There were reports coming in from all over. However, these are matters of national security, I cannot tell you more . . .'

Ironically, the man who was with Rajiv Gandhi when he took over as prime minister was dropped from his Cabinet just two months later. The seeds of doubt—Pranab Mukherjee as a possible contender to the role—sown by those close to Rajiv Gandhi after his mother's death had borne fruit. And history was destined to repeat itself. In 1991, seven years later, during his election campaign in Sriperumbudur, Tamil Nadu, Rajiv Gandhi was assassinated.

'It was a monumental tragedy,' says Pranab Mukherjee. 'In fact, I feel Rajiv Gandhi would have been a much better prime minister the second time around.'

'You are often described as the "best prime minister India never had". In 2004, when Sonia Gandhi led the party to victory against a formidable Atal Behari Vajpayee and then stepped aside, did you feel that you deserved the post as prime minister?' I ask.

'I criticized her, I disagreed with her strongly at the time,' Pranab says forthrightly. 'I didn't agree with her decision to step aside at all. I told her the mandate was for her, the mandate was not for her to appoint someone else in her place. She had no right to do that. She had taken her decision, however, and in that situation, Manmohan Singh was the best man for the job.'

In his memoir, *The Coalition Years, 1996–2012*, Pranab Mukherjee confesses that he had the impression that Sonia Gandhi had considered him as the prime ministerial candidate in 2004 and Manmohan Singh as a Presidential candidate. When this didn't happen, Pranab Mukherjee was reluctant to join the Manmohan Singh government, but was eventually prevailed upon, and he went on to become the main troubleshooter for the UPA government. Destiny, however, had other plans in store for him. In 2012, Pranab Mukherjee was elected to the Republic's highest constitutional post—the position he once thought Manmohan Singh may occupy—the President of India. This lifelong Congressman also swore in the first BJP prime minister to win with an absolute majority, and who, in turn, conferred him with the Bharat Ratna.

'The two prime ministers, Indira Gandhi and Narendra Modi, are often compared to each other. You've worked with one very closely and interacted with the other. Do you find any similarities?' I ask.

'They are more dissimilar than similar,' he replies. 'Indira Gandhi was secular to the last bone in her body. However, the one thing they share is political understanding. They have both visited Arunachal Pradesh twice as prime minister. Even though the state has only two seats, they did it because they have a national vision. They want to send a strong message to China. Their similarities end there.

'In fact, there will be no other prime minister like Pandit Nehru,' he says. 'I didn't have the honour of working with him, but he was a true champion of democracy like no other. Interestingly, Prime Minister Modi has taken two things from me—the idea of having

the budget coincide with the calendar year, I first set up a committee
regarding this in 1976. Also, the Goods and Service Tax [GST], I had
almost finalized it, in my term as finance minister; it was eventually
passed however in the Modi government, although I would have
done it very differently.' What Pranab Mukherjee diplomatically
leaves out though is that the GST didn't pass in his term because
then chief minister Modi and the BJP had all opposed it—this is all
politically water under the bridge now for him.

However, I point out to him, the most significant political
transition of our times has been not a change of government but the
BJP replacing the Congress as the central axis of national politics.
The other big transition in the larger political landscape has been the
shift from secularism to Hinduism, with even the Congress today
following the BJP in wearing a religious identity as a badge of honour.

'It's just temporary. India needs the Congress. Without the
Congress we will be Balkanized. I am convinced this will not be a
constant position,' Pranab Mukherjee responds emphatically.

'More importantly, Hinduism is the greatness, the vastness of
this country. It is a way of life, and it is inclusive. It cannot, and must
not, be brought into the competitive nature of politics. Doing so
will sully it. Do we want to be Pakistan? In the West, the American
President is sworn in with the Bible and in England, the monarch
does the same while swearing in the prime minister, but in India,
we use the Constitution. That is our holy book and secularism is the
cornerstone of our great Republic,' he concludes.

Yet, the ex-President chose to go against what his party had
publicly expressed, and go to the Rashtriya Swayamsevak Sangh
(RSS), the very antithesis, many would argue, of the views he has
just outlined. On 6 June 2018, Pranab Mukherjee's speech at the
RSS headquarters in Nagpur was broadcast live by every television
network. I was struck by the deftness with which he made a larger
political point as he quoted Jawaharlal Nehru—the Sangh's bête

noire—in their home ground with RSS chief Mohan Bhagwat listening intently. And that he did in quintessential Pranab style.

'Any attempt at defining our nationhood in terms of dogmas and identities of religion, region, hatred and intolerance will only lead to dilution of our national identity. It was this nationalism that Pandit Jawaharlal Nehru so vividly expressed in *The Discovery of India*, and I quote,' said Pranab Mukherjee in his speech, '"I am convinced that nationalism can only come out of the ideological fusion of Hindu, Muslim, Sikh, and other groups in India. That does not mean that extinction of any real culture of any group, but it does mean a common national outlook, to which other matters are subordinated."'

Pranab Mukherjee ended with, 'The soul of India resides in pluralism and tolerance. This plurality of our society has come through assimilation of ideas over centuries. Secularism and inclusion are a matter of faith for us. It is our composite culture which makes us into one nation.'

He smiles as he tells me, 'I wanted to go to the lion's den and show them where they are going wrong.'

And perhaps a larger message that couldn't have been lost on both the BJP and the Congress . . . He may have retired from political life, but you can't take the politician out of Pranab Mukherjee. As we end, I reflect, it is Pranab Mukherjee's sweeping overview of India's political and cultural history that is unparalleled today. His intellect and political understanding are a rarity in our times when political discourse has been debased—in that, he is a true Bharat Ratna.

[2]

Arun Jaitley

Democracy and Its Emergencies

There's an ironic symmetry to the fact that my next conversation in this book is with Arun Jaitley, an exact counterpoint to Pranab Mukherjee. One began his political career as an Indira protégé, the other came to political prominence when he was jailed for protesting against the Indira Emergency. Both have very different perspectives of the years that followed.

---

* Interview conducted on 7 March 2019, New Delhi

Today, in a room lined with books at his residence, sixty-six-year-old Finance Minister Arun Jaitley, the third most powerful man in the BJP, is busy troubleshooting with an ally on one phone and giving legal insight regarding a government matter on another while he keeps his focus on the strategic handling of the aftermath of the air strikes in Pakistan. Despite being struck by illness and not being able to present the Modi government's last budget before the 2019 elections, he remains in the thick of the political maelstrom. Yet he is also a leader whose vision isn't limited to a five-year canvas, and instead has been shaped by his vantage point in some of Indian democracy's key moments, from the Emergency onwards to Modi's landslide election victory in 2014 and now in redefining the rules of engagement with Pakistan.

'In the life of any country, the most defining moment is the creation of the country itself. That of course was the midnight of 15 August 1947. Perhaps if you look back over the last century, nobody can give another time besides 1947 as the defining moment, but since that is not in controversy, I would place three categories of defining moments in India—the first, relating to democracy; the second, relating to the economy; and the third, to security and sovereignty-related issues.

'Today,' he says,' the defining moment regarding India's sovereignty and security are the surgical strikes of 2016 and the air strikes at Balakot of 2019. India responded well over the past three decades in internationalizing Pakistan's role as the nerve centre of terror. However, India also conventionally maintained a policy dictated by foreign policy considerations that we must maintain the sanctity of both the international border and the Line of Control [LoC]. Since 1971, we had never crossed them. The terrorists breached the sanctity of both the international border and the LoC regularly. These terrorists are proxy for the Pakistan Army. We maintained the sanctity of the two. This was an uneven fight. Extraordinary situations require an out-of-box thinking. Conventionalists cannot find such solutions. India needed a leader who had fire in the belly and who could rise to the occasion. Prime Minister Narendra Modi is a leader with a difference. On this, both his admirers and critics agree. The surgical strikes of 2016 and the air strikes of 2019 changed India's approach. Terror must be attacked from where it originates. Otherwise, you will only be defending yourself against terror. You may succeed or may fail. The prime minister displayed decisiveness. Our army, in 2016, displayed the highest level of professionalism through surgical strikes wherein they destroyed terrorist camps next to the LoC. But the 2019 air strikes at Balakot was a daredevil operation of the Indian Air Force [IAF]. The air power was used to destroy the nerve centre of Jaish-e-Mohammed. The incorrigibles were taken by surprise. This marks a new approach of aggression in India's war against terror. We now bat on the front foot,' he says proudly.

'The stakes were extremely high,' I point out. 'Were you confident of the outcome especially when dealing with a nuclear nation?'

'Absolutely,' he says. 'I've always had full confidence in the professionalism and the assessment of the armed forces. This time, as well, they have more than adequately won the trust of the country, with our air force team coming back in such a short period of time with not even one casualty. Regarding Pakistan's nuclear bluff, will they use it to defend terrorists? We didn't attack Pakistan, we attacked terror.

'The other point,' Arun Jaitley continues, 'is that Kashmir is the unfinished agenda of Pakistan since Partition. Pakistan never reconciled to Kashmir being a part of India. The initial years of domination on the state's politics by Sheikh Abdullah and an erroneous Nehruvian vision of Kashmir made it worse for us. The very thought that a separate or special identity for the state will lead to a better integration has been proved wrong. The journey of separate status for seven decades has been towards separation and not for integration.

'Article 35A [a constitutional provision of 1954 which gives the Jammu and Kashmir assembly power to decide who are permanent residents of the state along with rights like buying property, government jobs, etc.] is a constitutional puzzle. It was not inserted in the Constitution by an amendment made by two Houses of Parliament with the support of a two-third majority. It was an executive insertion by Presidential Notification. It entered the Constitution through the back door. It contains a fundamental breach of the Right to Equality in as much as it promotes discrimination between two categories of citizens based on an irrational criterion. It is constitutionally vulnerable.'

This from the man who was one of India's top lawyers and is still the government's go-to person for all constitutional and legal issues is an important indication of what the Centre's thinking on this is. Petitions against Article 35A are currently pending in the Supreme Court.

Arun Jaitley says, 'The combination of a special status coupled with Article 35A acted against the interest of the people of Jammu and Kashmir. It prevented investment into the state. No major industries, no hotel chains, no private educational institutions, etc., came into the state. There was no specialized human resource from outside available for scientific research, management for hospitals and medical institutions and technical colleges. Why would anyone come to the state where he cannot own a house, his children cannot get admitted to government colleges, they cannot get a government job? The constitutional framework of the State hurt the people, but it satisfied the separatist psyche of some.

'Meanwhile, Pakistan tried conventional wars but lost out. In the last three decades it resorted to terror and insurgency organized and encouraged from across the border to create instability in the state. Democracy, secularism, and public order suffered. The people lived a life of insecurity because of terror. Governance and elections inevitably suffered in an atmosphere of fear. The entire Kashmiri Pandit community and most of the Sikhs were ostracized from the state. This was nothing short of ethnic cleansing. This is the single greatest failure of secularism in Independent India,' he says forcefully.

Today, he feels, is a decisive moment in addressing the entire Kashmir issue.

'The nation is now debating as to how to correct the Nehruvian blunder seven decades ago. Most Indians believe that Panditji's vision and formulation of Kashmir has proved to be disastrous. Seven decades' experience and the cost incurred stare us in the face. Our approach has to be guided by the principles of sovereignty coupled with keeping the welfare and security and interest of the Kashmiri people in mind. That dictates an aggressive posture against separatists and terrorists. What we are currently seeing is the attempt to establish a rule of law in the Valley. This is a decisive moment.'

A moment, however, where the government has been attacked for the rise in local unrest and the failure to hold state elections. And a time which requires rare unanimity among India's political class, an almost impossible task during election season. Perhaps, that is why in Arun Jaitley's opinion, the high point of Indian democracy was the adoption of the Constitution—a time when different strands of political opinion came together for an ideal larger than themselves.

He explains, 'Even though the Congress was the dominant party, the political leaders of that generation, besides being politicians, were of a much higher quality so you will find various viewpoints, tones of left- or right-wing thinking, Gandhians, community and regional interest being represented, yet you find all of them adopting one stand on sovereignty and, in those days, on sovereignty-related issues, the conservatism was far more than it is today. You also had a very high level of scholarship. If you see the quality of the debates itself, the language, the idioms used, they've lasted us for decades, and they brought out what was considered the best document made for India.

They realized that India needed democracy as the only system. The only consensus was parliamentary democracy, and that was a very wise decision because in a country with multiple regions, castes, religions, tribes, communities, eating habits, dress habits, everything being different, how do you ensure a system where every varied social, political, regional and community interest finds representation in the decision-making process?

'Since then, in our Parliament and legislative bodies, you'll find all kinds of opinions which are represented. And in the making of a decision process, of legislation, of policy, any decision maker, when in government, because you have to normally rule from the Centre, has to factor in those varied interests—equality, multiplicity of religions, fundamental rights, free and fair elections. Some of the institutions which we have created are dependent on that.'

More importantly he stresses that it is this constitutional democracy that was the key in determining how two new countries, born in 1947, have taken very different paths today.

'Pakistan and India were one nation before 1947. We strengthened democracy every day, made it more vibrant. Why did Pakistan fail? Why did they have martial law four times? We created an institution, and the most important factor, a very professional army. Our Election Commission under any government was always fair and highly trusted, theirs was accused of rigging elections; our judiciary, irrespective of the governments, was always fair and commanded trust, it never followed the ballot box or the government. It kept you guessing which way they are going till the last minute. There, you had multiple occasions where martial law was upheld, the execution of Zulfikar Ali Bhutto and many other judgments that followed during the Musharraf era. So, I think, in creating these institutions, this was a well-thought-of idea of democracy laid out in our Constitution.'

Since then, Arun Jaitley tells me, democracy in India has faced an existential challenge only once—when he witnessed it first-hand. In a sense, the young student leader's political coming-of-age happened during the Emergency. As the Akhil Bharatiya Vidyarthi

Parishad (ABVP) head, a right-wing all-India student organization affiliated with the RSS, and a Delhi University student, he was busy organizing student agitations and demonstrations of Opposition leaders from Atal Behari Vajpayee and L.K. Advani in Delhi to JP (freedom fighter and political idealist, Jayaprakash Narayan was the man who became the face of the anti-Indira movement) in Patna when the Emergency was announced.

'The only real threat to democracy in India came in 1975. The ultimate experience of the 1975 Emergency and the consequence was such that nobody will ever dare repeat it. You used a democratic instrument—the Constitution and the Emergency provisions under it—to subvert the Constitution from within; you suspended fundamental rights; and scared the courts into delivering a judgment. This was the only time in recent history where the courts have been, or at least the Supreme Court became subjugated to the government. You detained people and there is no remedy in the law even if it is an illegal detention; you censored the press, you virtually had a Parliament without an opposition,' Arun Jaitley recounts animatedly.

'After the 1971 elections and the Bangladesh victory, Indira Gandhi was an all-powerful prime minister like Prime Minister Modi post 2014 and now after the strikes as well. How did the Opposition and people's anger start building up?' I ask.

'After Indira Gandhi won the 1971 elections, she wanted the accumulation of all power,' he replies.

'Indira Gandhi seemed invincible in 1971, but more so in 1972 in the state assemblies because of the Bangladesh victory. The 1971 election was pre-Bangladesh but the Bangladesh liberation strengthened her position. It is a lesson for all Indians in politics,' he says. 'From 1972 and absolute invincibility, she became highly unpopular by 1974. Do you know the rate of inflation in 1975? It was 24 per cent—that's something which is incredible to believe now. What was the meaning of the economic reforms started in 1991? To undo most of what she did.'

Indira Gandhi nationalized food grain trade, insurance, and every conceivable industry, such as coal mining, so that there was no investment in these areas. There were no jobs left except in the public sector. So, the commanding heights of the public sector meant that the government had very little resources; whatever the government put into manufacturing units of the public sector was the only economic activity, otherwise it didn't take place. There was inflation, unemployment—it just needed to be flared. How did it get flared?

'In 1974, in Ahmedabad, there was an engineering college called LD Engineering College. Because of the inflation, food and edible oil prices went up. The college had to substantially increase the hostel charges and those children came out on to the streets in protest. Then, this spread to students in the next hostel and within two or three days, the whole of Gujarat had lakhs and lakhs of people on the roads. No jobs, high prices, fees went up, hostel charges went up and then it flared up in Patna. Soon, government employees weren't getting raises because of the poor economic situation. So, bad economic policies led to bad governance and increasing socio-economic discontent and it was most evident in 1974 when the railways strike took place organized by George Fernandes.'

As the political tension increased, even student elections saw a prime minister address a campaign rally. Arun Jaitley vividly describes the atmosphere back then.

'In Delhi, I was the president of the students' union, and Mrs Gandhi had come and addressed a Delhi University youth rally at India Gate's boat club lawns. I announced that if I win in the university campus, JP will come and speak. So, when JP came and stood in Maurice Nagar and delivered a speech, on all the three sides, from St Stephen's college you could only see students on hostel tops, building tops, trees, streets—it had become a very tense political environment. So, if anybody is to take a lesson on how to lose popularity the 1972–74 period is the best-case study since Independence.'

'Many today, especially the Opposition, would draw parallels with what you are saying and the current situation with Prime Minister Modi. They call it an undeclared emergency,' I say.

His rebuttal is swift. 'Forget prime ministers, even governments don't have absolute power today. The media, NGOs, civil society, political parties, public opinion, and even the Opposition, has power. The judiciary has the power. A civil servant can say, I don't agree, and make you rethink a decision, so even within a democratic system, these are the internal checks and balances because there's a spread of power in democracy. The Indira Gandhi government's attitude was, "What is this institution? We are the elected people. The Parliament is sovereign and since we have a majority in the Parliament, we should be allowed to do anything, even superseding judges and appointing those friendly to the government." The election law was also amended retrospectively, to get her election declared valid.

'A plan was then put in place,' says Arun Jaitley. 'Once we detain all the Opposition leaders, there is no Opposition left, Parliament is completely without an Opposition, you can pass anything and can amend the Constitution and make all kinds of laws.'

When these developments were taking place, the young Arun Jaitley invited JP for the second time to Delhi University and called student leaders from across the country. This included a fascinating list—Lalu Yadav, Sushil Modi, current Jammu and Kashmir Governor Satyapal Malik and the current vice president Venkaiah Naidu. Arun Jaitley was the convener of the committee appointed and he had the opportunity to travel with JP across the country, where the crowds supporting him and his slogan 'Sampoorna Kranti' or 'Complete Revolution' were growing. It was in this charged atmosphere that came the fateful midnight knock.

'When the Emergency was proclaimed at midnight on 25 June 1975, they came to arrest me. I managed to escape by going to a friend's house nearby. They took my father instead but released him subsequently. The next morning the university was closed since it was June. So, I collected as many people as I could and burnt an effigy of Mrs Gandhi and got arrested. I courted arrest. I technically became the first "satyagrahi" against the Emergency because on 26 June, this was the only protest in the country. For three months, I was at Ambala Jail.'

However, the law student decided to make the best of his time as a political prisoner.

'I must confess it was in jail that I picked up an aptitude for reading and writing. Friends and family would send me books or I would borrow them from the jail library; its librarian was a very eminent man. He was Delhi's best-known ophthalmologist and eye surgeon, Dr N.S. Jain, who was in prison for having killed his wife. Occasionally, I wrote pamphlets that used to be translated into Hindi and sent out.'

'How did jail change you?' I ask.

'Jail is a state of mind,' he replies. 'If you have a lot of liabilities outside, like family, livelihood issues and so on, then it worries you and kills you. We were young students, we had no such problems. Both my sisters were married, my father was a lawyer and my parents lived by themselves. So, I thought either I live with my parents and complete my studies, or I live here in jail. If you have nerves of steel, you can take it. At that time, we lived as a middle-class family in an India where the living conditions had not made us very vulnerable. Those were the days without an AC, so you had to sleep under a fan, or sleep on the terrace. That's what we did in prison. If you feel like you're a part of an ideological struggle and you're fighting for democracy, then that gives you a sense of pride about what you're doing. It also gives you an opportunity to shape your own ideas. For instance, I read the entire Constituent Assembly debates in jail. I would read a lot, write occasionally, and that's a passion that's continued. On a lighter side, morning and evening we would play badminton and volleyball.'

The one thing the young man from a Punjabi household used to good food found difficult, however, were the jail rations—a deprivation he's done his best to make up for since then. The quality of food at regular Jaitley lunches are legendary, as is his fondness for butter chicken at Delhi's Moti Mahal.

'The jail food used to be very bad. As a detainee, you'd get a fixed ration allowance—a total of Rs 3. After an agitation, it was increased to Rs 5, which wasn't as bad as it is today. But you could afford a chapati and a vegetable at one time and a chapati and a dal in the next meal—these were the only two meals possible. Additionally, you'd use various techniques to improvise. All of us faked illness so we could get a medical diet of eggs, bread and butter which used to suffice as breakfast. Secondly, they had instituted false cases against us, so we didn't take bail on those cases, so, the trials would go on and on. When we'd go to court in a jail van, our family or friends would wait for us to hand over cooked food, and I would come back holding tiffins of food in both hands for my co-detainees. Earlier, no meetings with family was allowed but after a few months, they were allowed to visit once a month, then once a week. We shared it. Monday—your family will come, Tuesday—your family will come, and so on. Each family was instructed to bring some add-ons. Plus, I used to supervise the kitchen, and that is where I picked up an aptitude for good food. You see, you organize parathas for breakfast. For the non-vegetarians we'd slip some money to the jail guard who would bring us some lamb or chicken, and we'd cook it there. So, we made the best of the Rs 5 and improved upon it.' Arun Jaitley smiles.

'A silver lining there to nineteen months in a prison cell,' I say. 'But what, according to you, are the larger lessons you and India learnt from the Emergency?'

He replies after a pause. 'If you ask me, the most worrisome parts of the Emergency were three: you could use a constitutional provision to subvert the Constitution; when the prime minister turns dictatorial, the whole government machinery accedes, not a single police officer in the country said, "I won't file a fake FIR." I had seven FIRs against me for giving a speech at 4 a.m., that I wanted to overthrow the government, those kind of FIRs, but they were all fake. Not a single district magistrate got up and said, "I won't sign a false detention order"—this is worrisome; and finally, except political workers, the judiciary, media, civil service, and civil society, all other institutions collapsed.'

Listening to Arun Jaitley relive his Emergency days forty-four years later is fascinating, especially as he is such a strong critic of Indira Gandhi, yet it is to her that Prime Minister Narendra Modi is most often compared in the sense that both are seen as strong, autocratic leaders, in complete command of their parties and governments. 'If Indira Gandhi was the Congress, Narendra Modi is the BJP,' I state.

'No, I think it's a larger issue,' he says. 'There's a changed world order taking place. That global change is—you experimented in all liberal democracies with moderate leaders, power-sharing, and consensus-based politics. Post the Second World War, this was the pattern of liberal democracies. Over the last decade and a little more, it's changing. In the initial phases, there was only one exception: Margaret Thatcher. But otherwise till the 1990s, the post-War experience of liberal democracies was moderate leaders and consensus-based politics and that led to weakening the decision-making process. Today, look at the strong leaders around the world—Angela Merkel—look at the US and Turkey. Look at how Theresa May's politics depends on whether she sticks to her guns and delivers. If she delivers, the entire world perception will be that she's going the Thatcher way. Even where she can't carry her whole party with her, she is not going in for consensus. Look at Japan. The global model in democracies today suggests there is an evolutionary change happening all over the world.'

Linking this trend to India, Arun Jaitley continues, 'What led to our failing in the UPA-2? Parallel power centres, a prime minister in power, in office but not in power, policy paralysis—the reaction to that had to be a strong and decisive leader. But a strong and decisive leader doesn't mean you're an autocracy. Your democratic systems and institutions will work, but this is an evolution that must play out. Democracies themselves are now trying this alternative model,' he says, placing the Modi style of leadership as part of a larger global change.

Moving to the economy, the current finance minister chooses what he sees as the defining change, 1991 and the economic reforms under Prime Minister Narasimha Rao, outlined by then finance minister Manmohan Singh.

'If you look at the growth rate from 1947 to 1991—what was called a Hindu rate of growth—there was no entrepreneurship, no opportunities. I grew up in that period and I know India was a land of shortages. If you went to a telephone exchange, the waiting list used to be twenty-two years for a phone. Members of Parliament used to be given one scooter to be allotted out of turn, some phones to be allotted out of turn and two HMT watches to be allotted out of turn because everything was scarce. I think 1991 changed that and now it's changing for the better every day. I'll leave it at that.'

I find it interesting that Arun Jaitley doesn't choose demonetization as a defining moment of India's economic history.

'It was a part of several steps we took to reduce black money, increase tax base, and digitalization,' he says but doesn't go further.

'However,' he continues, 'instrumental in changing the entire character of Indian politics has been the Mandal Commission.[†] Mandal is a positive step from a social-justice point of view but it also became a very powerful political instrument. The BJP had

---

[†] The commission was headed by Bihar MP B.P. Mandal to consider the issue of reservations. Its report accepted by the V.P. Singh government in 1990 said that 52 per cent of India's population belonged to socially or educationally backward classes and recommended reservations of 27 per cent government jobs for the OBCs. This led to widespread demonstrations across India. Opponents said Mandal signaled the death of merit.

already seen this trend being created so even at the cost of losing urban support, the BJP supported the Mandal recommendations. The BJP always, as a rule, gave preference to OBCs [Other Backward Classes] as chief ministers.'

'As a young, urban-educated lawyer, did you support it?' I ask.

'At that time, I was also a politician and we realized that while there may be reservations about some communities still being included in the OBC list but in the case of scheduled castes and scheduled tribes for sure, and the OBCs, to a large extent, reservations are still required. In OBCs, you require a change where you must ensure that the "creamy layer" principle effectively allows this to penetrate to the weakest in the OBCs, so broadly if you ask me, the answer is, yes, I did support Mandal.'

This created a divide in the party's urban base however, with young Delhi University students from other castes even setting themselves on fire to protest against Mandal.

'Delhi's urban mood was anti-Mandal,' Arun Jaitley points out, 'and, therefore, we were all at the receiving end when we supported it. However, captured by the Lutyens mood, Rajiv Gandhi made a fatal mistake. On 6 September 1990, he delivered his longest, and Congressmen call it his best-ever, speech, lasting three hours in Parliament. He tore Mandal into pieces and the Congress for the next few generations lost the OBCs' support. One speech cost the Congress the OBCs. The Congress as a party from 300 to 400 seats, it was the umbrella organization, the rainbow coalition within the Congress—*woh post-Mandal India mein 100 to 150 seat ki party ban gayi*. Rajiv Gandhi's one fatal mistake cost the Congress the whole election. The BJP, meanwhile, supported Mandal. Vajpayeeji and Advaniji had stones thrown at them when they went to Safdarjung hospital to meet anti-Mandal protestors who had immolated themselves. We took a decision that day though, I remember, I was in the meeting and we still went ahead and appointed Kalyan Singh, Shivraj Singh Chouhan, Narendra Modi, all OBCs, as chief ministers of key heartland states. Indian politics, as we knew it, changed and the change was in two ways.

'One, the impact of Mandal on social justice was positive but its impact on politics was not so. In fact, at times, it was adverse. Post-Mandal, political parties in India became caste-based. A family with a leader and an inheritance and ownership of the party within the family became the rule. This had a demonstrative effect even on the non-Mandal parties. If you look at People's Democratic Party [PDP], National Conference [NC], Akali Dal, Samajwadi Party [SP], Dravida Munnetra Kazhagam [DMK], maybe on a future date, even Bahujan Samaj Party [BSP], Rashtriya Janata Dal [RJD], maybe Trinamool, Biju Janata Dal [BJD], this new Telangana Rashtra Samithi [TRS]. All post-Mandal parties followed the Congress principle of dynasty, some because of Mandal and others because of the demonstration effect. *Power family mein rakhna hain* [To keep political power in the family] and the leader is the symbol of the caste. *Politics, yeh hai ki bhai, jeetne ke liye, apni caste toh aa gayi, ek aur jodlo* [To win, you must have the support of your own caste and then add more castes in support] so you can get a bouquet. You need multiple flowers in a bouquet, this kind of alliance started taking place from place to place. Now, when these combinations come to power, the quality of governance is very poor.

'However, Mandal had a positive impact on empowerment, both political, economic, jobs wise, and educationally. For instance, I asked in the SRCC governing body what was the cut-off, they said 97.75 per cent, so I asked what was the OBC cut-off, they said 96 per cent. So the gap is so narrow now so there is an empowerment in the OBCs, it's a positive step. In the nature of political parties and the quality of governance, however, it is not a positive step.'

Politically, the BJP also learnt another important lesson: the importance of a core ideology.

'We learnt a lesson in the 1980s. Even when we lost, we stuck to our ideological position and rebuilt, 2 to 89 to 126 to 163 to 183.

Our isolation was completed and then today we occupy a pivotal position in politics. And in the 1990s we became a bipolar system. The Congress never stuck to its ideological position. I delivered a Vajpayee memorial lecture [Arun Jaitley first became minister in the Vajpayee Cabinet] on what was the ex–prime minister's key contribution. If I had to select one, I said, he took an ideological position even when there were only four MPs, he took an ideological position even when there were only two MPs and from a non-starter, he went on in the 1990s, he created a party and finally, by the time he retired, in his last ten years, he made it a centre-stage party. So, he made Indian politics bipolar. If India had not become bipolar, the communists would have withered away—they are globally irrelevant. You'd have small regional parties and you'd have a monolith of the Congress. Since the Congress was dynastic, and the regional parties could never have gotten together to challenge the experiment. But for this contribution of Mr Vajpayee, India wouldn't have become a bipolar political system and virtually been under a dynastic party. Unipolar and probably more akin to a kingdom,' he states.

'Have we also now seen a shift politically from what was once called minority politics to majority politics in India?' I point out. 'Are we now socially a different country post 2014?'

'There are two trends,' Arun Jaitley responds. 'Muslims, in particular, were being told they are the vote balancer. If you overuse that card, then you must remember that everybody has a vote. Muslims aren't the only ones with a vote. A reaction against such politics was seen in 2014,' he says tersely, a reference to the fact that in a shift from traditional caste-based and minority votes, there was a consolidation of what analysts call a 'Hindu' vote to the BJP leading to their record 282 seats.

'Having said this, I am making a prediction. I am seeing in my day-to-day life, in urban India, in the metropolitan cities, caste and religion differences have substantially come down. Every invitation I am getting for a wedding this season, the girls are working, they choose their spouses themselves, parents are agreeing. I can see caste completely collapsing in metropolitan India. It is now going to move to tier-two, tier-three cities. In metropolitan cities, caste is collapsing, regional differences are narrowing and even inter-religion marriages are becoming visible. I can see an exponential growth in India's middle class. Women are getting into formal employment and many more will take their own personal decisions. Within my family, social circle and even amongst the political class, this trend is increasing. It will still take some time for rural India to accept this. Even amongst the Muslims, I can now see a middle and aspirational class grow. The bread-and-butter issues will be primary.'

Would the hardliners in his party agree, though? 'Will that mean an end to mandir–masjid politics?' I ask.

He replies, 'For extremely sentimental issues you have to be pragmatic. Ram Mandir is a hugely aspirational issue of the majority community. For example, if you see, agitations have disappeared, and to get a crowd of 5000 people is becoming impossible to organize. Protests are of a very small size; now you take your grievances out on Twitter. I see a situation emerging in twenty-five years, when the middle class will be the dominant class. Therefore, the character of politics will completely change and for parties to survive only on caste or religion will be difficult. Performance and governance will matter.'

An India where politics has moved beyond caste and religion—a hope for the future shared by one of India's most powerful and erudite politicians.

[3]

The Dalai Lama

A Lifetime of Exile

Arriving in McLeod Ganj in Dharamshala—where 'The Living Buddha,' which is what the incarnation of the fourteenth Dalai Lama is revered as, lives in exile—you can immediately sense how his presence here has diffused like a fragrance into the mountain air. A serene calm, unlike in any other Indian mountain town, surrounds you. Here, tourists, Israeli backpackers and Buddhist monks all blend into a landscape dominated by a busy, thriving Tibetan community settled around their lodestar: the Dalai Lama. At eighty-three years old, he is one of the world's most respected spiritual leaders. The title—the 'Dalai Lama'—literally means Ocean of Wisdom, yet he describes himself as a simple Buddhist monk and above all, a human being.*

---

* Interview conducted on 12 October 2018, Dharamshala

As I enter the Dalai Lama's residence, where hundreds are gathered outside reverentially for a public audience, I try to imagine what it must have been like for a young man albeit a 'God King, the political and spiritual leader of the Tibetan people', who was only twenty-three years old, to leave his precious Tibet for India. He had left behind the ancient land of Lhasa where he had lived in the grand Potala Palace, a palatial residence of over a thousand rooms, to come to this modest yet beautiful home surrounded by deodar trees and the magnificent Himalayas.

It is this journey from the Tibetan mountains to the foothills of the Himalayas that the Dalai Lama tells me about. This is also the story of his journey from being a Tibetan Buddhist religious icon and the temporal head of the Tibetan government to becoming the world's most prominent exile, a Nobel Laureate for Peace, and still the primary enemy for the Chinese.

Even today, sixty years later, the dramatic events leading to his escape are fresh in his mind. In a political manoeuvre led by Chairman Mao of the Communist Chinese government of the People's Republic of China, the People's Liberation Army entered Tibet in October 1950, easily outnumbering the small, ill-equipped Tibetan army. A month later, the fifteen-year-old Dalai Lama was hurriedly anointed the temporal and spiritual leader of the Tibetan people. The world, including India, refused to meet Tibetan delegations seeking assistance at the time. Within a few months, the Chinese occupation of Tibet was a reality with some promise of Tibetan autonomy. In the years that followed, however, the on-ground situation changed rapidly even as the Dalai Lama travelled to Peking and India to meet with the leadership of both countries. In 1954 and 1956, he met with Chairman Mao. In 1956, the Dalai Lama visited India to attend the 2500th Buddha Jayanti celebrations. There, he met Jawaharlal Nehru who advised him to return to Lhasa, and work with the Chinese on the basis of the seventeen-point agreement. The young Dalai Lama, hopeful he would be able to forge a better understanding with the Chinese for his people, did just that.

However, the moment of reckoning was nearing as the Chinese gradually began to exert their authority over the Tibetan people. In March 1959, the Dalai Lama was faced with a stark choice: flee or be held captive, and maybe killed.

'I had received an invitation from the Chinese to view a dance performance of a new Chinese troupe at their military headquarters in Lhasa,' he remembers. 'They wanted me to come with only a few unarmed bodyguards—no Tibetan soldiers—and that the matter should be kept completely secret. I accepted the invitation to avoid any diplomatic unpleasantness with the Chinese. But the news about this meeting spread rapidly. Thousands of people began marching to my summer palace, the Norbulingka, and by the afternoon of 10 March 1959, the day when I was meant to attend the performance, the entire palace was surrounded by an estimated thirty thousand Tibetans for my protection. They refused to let me leave for the military headquarters and would not move from their position in the fear that I would be attacked by the Chinese. I tried my best to calm the situation but the standoff continued,' His Holiness recounts calmly. A young man in his twenties, guarded by just the devotion of his people, unarmed against the powerful Chinese military. Yet, there was more to come.

'Every night from my room, we could hear the movement of trucks—always with guns, big guns on the long road from Amdo to Lhasa. On 16 March, I received word from the Chinese to identify on a map my exact location, so that they could protect the palace wing I was staying in. However, what was the real intention of them asking me to do so?' he asks me. 'To protect the palace I was in or target it?'

The Dalai Lama was faced with a crucial dilemma, but divine intervention also played a role. Through the tumultuous events of March, he had consulted with the Nechung, the State Oracle, about whether he should escape or stay. Each time, the Oracle told him to stay and continue dialogue with the Chinese.

'However, the situation was different that day,' narrates the Dalai Lama. 'I called the Oracle again once I had learnt of the Chinese plan to target the palace. And he asked me to leave immediately. The decision was taken in a matter of hours. The next day, at 10 p.m., I left Norbulingka uncertain if I would ever live to see the next day.'

Dressed in trousers and a black coat, instead of his ceremonial robes, his trademark spectacles in his pocket (which meant he could barely see anything), a rifle slung over his shoulder and little else, the disguised fourteenth Dalai Lama left his summer palace, where the Tibetan heads of state had lived for centuries, with just a small entourage of people.

'Our journey was riddled with the fear that the Chinese would, at any moment, discover our ploy,' he says. 'But, the next morning, we reached the Che La mountain pass that separates the Lhasa valley from the Tsangpo valley. This was the last point from which I could see Lhasa. My bodyguard escort turned my horse around to see my beloved home for the last time, and I said one last prayer and left,' he tells me calmly, the memory still fresh in his mind.

'Throughout the journey I was accompanied by fear and the feeling of responsibility, that this was not just about me as an individual. The Dalai Lama's life is very important to the Tibetan people,' he says. 'On 20 March, I received news that artillery shells had bombed the palaces of Norbulingka and Potala.'

'So, if you hadn't left then, it is unlikely you would have been alive . . .' I say, the full impact of that momentous decision by the young Dalai Lama sinking in. He doesn't answer this directly as he continues to describe his journey of six decades ago.

'Well, our original route to get to India was through the western side of Tibet. But we realized that this region was packed with Chinese troops. So, we hurriedly decided to go via southern Tibet where there were no Chinese soldiers. But we were still not sure whether the Indian government would allow me into their country,' he says, since when the Dalai Lama had met Pandit Nehru in India in 1956, he had been told point-blank he should return to Tibet and work with the Chinese.

'So, we sent two delegations—one to the Indians and another to the Bhutanese. Then, we received information that the Indians were ready to receive me, so we could go to India straight away,' he says. 'As we crossed over into India, a small group of people, which included Indian officials I had known earlier, was there to meet me, and my immediate emotion as I touched foot on Indian soil was the feeling of safety.'

'I was taken to Mussoorie and a few days later, Pandit Nehru came to meet me. This time around, he showed great sympathy and concern for me. In the months after my arrival in 1959, an estimated total of 80,000 refugees, Tibetans from central Tibet and monks, all followed me to India and they all found sanctuary here,' the Dalai Lama reminisces.

'Tell me more about your relationship with Pandit Nehru,' I ask. 'Especially since he wasn't a supporter of an independent Tibet, as you have mentioned in your autobiography, *Freedom in Exile*; that he would often almost scold you as a young man. Yet, he also gave sanctuary not just to you but thousands of Tibetan refugees.'

The Dalai Lama breaks into his trademark laughter. 'Yes,' he says. 'After we had fled, we heard that the Chinese government had decided to dissolve the Tibetan government. So, we decided to set up a Tibetan government in southern Tibet and I reported this development to Nehru. He lost his temper with me, saying India cannot recognize our government. Immediately, he found a contradiction: "On one hand, you're very much concerned about peace in Lhasa," he told me, "at the same time, you also want to create a Tibetan government in southern Tibet." So, he wasn't very happy with me. However, he helped us as much as he could, in the maximum way possible.

'In October 1959, we also tried to raise the Tibet issue at the United Nations. I requested Pandit Nehru, "Please if possible—can India sponsor the UN resolution, if India can't do that, will it support the resolution?" Pandit Nehru refused saying, "No use!" Then, on one occasion, I told him that we were not expecting results immediately but that we must keep the Tibet issue alive. Pandit Nehru replied, "The proper way to keep the Tibet issue alive is to educate young Tibetans." Since we have our own language, I asked for separate Tibetan schools where there were large settlements of Tibetan refugees in India, which he immediately supported.'

'In fact,' I say, 'you have told me that Pandit Nehru defied his own ministers to give you refuge in India; they felt India shouldn't take sides by giving you shelter, especially as we had signed the Panchsheel agreement with China, which recognized Tibet as under the control of China.'

'Yes,' he agrees. 'The then Deputy Foreign Secretary Jagat Mehta, several years after he retired, came here especially to meet me and told me before his death that he wanted me to know about an event that had taken place many years ago. In 1959, after I escaped, the Indian mission in Lhasa sent a message to New Delhi—the Dalai Lama has left Norbulingka. In the Cabinet meeting that followed, the then defence minister Krishna Menon had said, "Oh, we shouldn't accept the Dalai Lama." Pandit Nehru immediately rejected this and said we must accept the Dalai Lama as a refugee.'

Given that this scenario took place when the Dalai Lama was still in his twenties and Pandit Nehru was in his late sixties, his insights into Pandit Nehru are fascinating. In fact, he has the rare perspective of having interacted with every prime minister of independent India. Intrigued by these personal interactions with political leaders, I ask,

'What have your impressions been of our country's leaders, from Pandit Nehru to Prime Minister Modi?'

'After the 1962 Sino-Indian War, where Indian troops were defeated, Pandit Nehru was extremely shocked at the outcome. My last meeting with him was just before he left for Dehradun, where he died a week later in May 1964. He was physically very weak. Indira Gandhi was also there, and I told her that her father's condition was very serious. Later, Mrs Gandhi told me that I must have had a premonition her father was going to die. My relationship with Indira Gandhi was very good, though she also was very sensitive about not being seen as pro-Tibet in order not to upset India's relationship with China. Indira Gandhi said to me, "We all want independence for Tibet, but we must also realize today's reality." She was frank and very sympathetic.

'Then Pandit Nehru's successor, Lal Bahadur Shastri, was wonderful, really. During his period, as prime minister from 1964–66, at one time, he was seriously thinking of recognizing the exiled Tibetan government. He was physically very small, but his mind was very bold. I think his sudden death in Russia in 1966 was a great tragedy,' muses the Dalai Lama. Continuing his recall of India's prime ministers, he adds, 'Narasimha Rao was also very good. One day he explained to me the Indian government policy—"We never say 'Tibet is a part of China'; we say, 'Tibet is an autonomous region of the People's Republic of China," he said.'

Prime ministers will change but it's clear that India has always walked a very careful tightrope with China on the Tibet question. 'Prime Minister Modi has looked at redefining India's relationship with China and you have enjoyed greater visibility under his government with your visit to Arunachal Pradesh and the Tawang monastery. Yet, "thank you" celebrations to mark your sixty years in India had to be shifted from Delhi to Dharamshala to avoid angering the Chinese. How has dealing with Prime Minister Modi been?' I ask.

'Awkward,' says the Dalai Lama wryly, then adding, 'And it's only natural, understandable. The China–India relationship is very important. When the Doklam problem happened [in 2017, China tried to build a road in Doklam, a stretch in Bhutan bordering India and China, to which India and Bhutan objected, resulting in a standoff], the media asked me about my beliefs and I told them that these were minor; neither India nor China want to destroy one another—we have to live side by side. The ultimate goal should be "Hindi–Chini bhai–bhai!" That is the only realistic way.

'So, naturally Prime Minister Modi is concerned about good relations with China. I actually know him very well. When he was the chief minister of Gujarat, the state found an ancient Buddhist monastery and as chief minister, Mr Modi invited me to a function for this. Besides the official meeting, he also came to see me at my hotel. We have very good relations. He is quite an active Indian prime minister, continuously visiting many countries. That, I admire at his age.'

And it is then as we talk of the prime minister that the Dalai Lama drops his political bombshell. 'In 2014, when Chinese President Xi Jinping visited Delhi for talks with Prime Minister Modi, I requested a meeting with him. President Xi Jinping agreed, but the Indian government was cautious about the meeting, so it didn't happen.'

Just like the historic moment between the heads of North Korea and South Korea in 2018, this could have been a meeting that had the promise to change the course of China–Tibet relations, especially as there have been reports that there are informal contacts between both sides. President Xi is said to have a close knowledge of Buddhism through his father who headed the Communist Party's religious work in 1980. During his stint as a young provincial officer as well in 1982, Xi Jinping was posted in Zhengding, China where he backed a Buddhist monk's efforts to rebuild the famous

Linji Temple and has asked workers to study the partnership between party and religion. In 2014, in a speech in Delhi, the Dalai Lama had said that President Xi was the first Chinese leader to publicly say that Buddhism had a role to play in the preservation of Chinese culture.[†]

However, a meeting between the Dalai Lama and President Xi could have also been used as a propaganda tool by the Chinese to outwit both India and the Dalai Lama, who is seen by some foreign policy strategists as India's trump card against the Chinese. It's not surprising then that the request for the meeting must have sent the ministry of external affairs into a spin leading to a denial of the request.

The Dalai Lama and his aides smile sagely but refuse to say anything more on this.

Perhaps, the Dalai Lama knows that this chapter will never be opened in his lifetime, especially after China's renewed hardened stand in the latest party Congress against him. Indo-China relations also currently remain at status quo after the Doklam situation diffused and India at the moment seems keen to avoid bringing the Dalai Lama into greater prominence.

I switch gears. 'What do you think, Your Holiness, India's policy should be for refugees, whether it's the Rohingyas or Bangladeshi Muslims? Where would Tibetan refugees have been today if India had turned its back on them?'

The Dalai Lama thinks carefully before answering the question. Even a Nobel Laureate for Peace must tread with caution sometimes, especially since he has been criticized for not adequately condemning the situation in Buddhist Myanmar which has driven out Rohingya Muslim refugees. 'I think India is wonderful,' he says. 'When

---

[†] https://economictimes.indiatimes.com/news/politics-and-nation/ chinese-president-xi-jinping-accepts-role-of-buddhism-in-their-culture- dalai-lama/articleshow/43155391.cms

Bangladeshi refugees come, India opens its arms. So, we will see. This is the most populated democratic country in the world, and I admire the thousands-year-old Indian tradition of spiritual knowledge and its influence on the mind and emotions. I am fully convinced that if we practise this knowledge, we will keep our confidence and will power.

'Take, for example, America,' he continues. 'A powerful nation like that will definitely draw people in desperate situations, like the Mexican refugees, to it. Instead, their President talks of building a wall. As human brothers and sisters, we should open our arms to those in need. Despite the overwhelming numbers, these refugees should be given shelter and provided all the facilities for the education of young people, be given the opportunity for training them in different skills. Similarly, in Europe, too. But refugees shouldn't remain in other countries permanently. Eventually, they should return to their own land and rebuild their own country.'

It's poignant to hear the Dalai Lama talk of going back, of returning to one's own country. 'You are Tibet's most visible symbol, but it may well be that you will not return to your homeland in this lifetime. Do you ever yearn to go back home, to die at home?' I ask gently.

'India is, spiritually and mentally, my real home,' he replies. 'It's only a different country physically. In 1973, during my first visit to Europe, I developed the concept of global responsibility. Thinking only of your own country is selfish; we must think for humanity. So, I try to talk about this sense of global responsibility at every opportunity I get. However, I too realized the power of ancient Indian knowledge can be beneficial to humanity. There is the Tibetan tradition, the Buddhist tradition; previously some people have described Lamaism saying this is not genuine Buddhism. Why does some stupid Lama [he laughs referring to himself] carry some strange weight? Even today, we have corrupted Lamas. They create a wrong impression. Lamaism isn't true Buddhism. People realize now that the Buddhist tradition is the authentic Nalanda tradition. Many Chinese Buddhists also now realize Tibetan Buddhism is based on the Nalanda tradition; it's a very scientific tradition.[‡]

'So, in a way, you've accepted that Tibet lives in your mind and heart, but you will never see it again?' I ask.

'Firstly, I always think of myself as a human being,' he replies. 'I am one human being amongst 7 billion. I believe in the oneness of humanity. There may be differences at the national level but that is minor. What's important is that your life should be useful. In my life, if returning to Tibet or China is useful, then okay, I will do so. But if it is not, then I'd prefer to stay in India.'

At eighty-three, however, questions about his health and succession are inevitable. China has already declared that the next Dalai Lama will be chosen from Tibet under Chinese control. 'Where do you think the next Dalai Lama will come from?' I ask.

'That is not my concern,' he replies tersely. 'There is a meeting of Tibetan High Lamas soon, at that time a discussion may happen.'[§]

'But will *you* accept a Chinese Dalai Lama? Or do you think the Tibetan people will accept a Chinese Dalai Lama?' I persist.

He dismisses it immediately. 'I don't think so. No one can accept a Chinese Dalai Lama. Look at what happened with the Panchen Lama recognized by Beijing.'[¶]

[‡]   Buddhism was introduced in Tibet by masters from the Nalanda monastery in Bihar. The root texts are based on Indian Sanskrit Buddhist texts and the focus is more on philosophical reason and logic rather than just faith.

[§]   It is believed that the Dalai Lamas are reincarnated. They are found by Tibetan High Lamas and the government through a 'search process' based on a vison that can come to the Lamas after meditation.

[¶]   The Dalai Lama had declared a six-year-old boy as the Panchen Lama, the second most revered figure in Tibetan Buddhism, in 1995. Chinese authorities detained him three days later and he hasn't been seen since. Instead, the Chinese appointed their own Panchen Lama who is not accepted by the Dalai Lama and the Tibetan community here.

'Finally,' I ask. 'The Chinese have referred to you as a "devil", while others consider you a "God-king." How would you like to be remembered?'

'Just a human being,' he says with a smile. 'When I received the Nobel Peace Prize in 1989, in my acceptance speech, I said that I am just a simple Buddhist monk, no more, no less.' He smiles and clasps my hands as he leaves me with these farewell words. I watch him go, people bowing in reverence as he passes.

Words of infinite wisdom from a Buddhist monk, revered as the reincarnation of Avalokiteshvara, the Bodhisattva of Compassion; yet the Dalai Lama is a spiritual leader who remains intrinsically political by his very being as a Tibetan religious leader. He is the most visible global ambassador for his people and the essential human values of compassion and non-violence. India gave him refuge as he fled his homeland to safety, but sixty years later, it is his very presence here today that has indeed enriched India.

[4]

Nirmala Sitharaman

In the Frontline of India's Defence

*Nirmala Sitharaman, India's first full-time woman defence minister (Indira Gandhi had held the portfolio from 1980–82 when she was prime minister), is in charge at a critical time for India—when India has signaled a major strategic shift by literally crossing the Line of Control (LoC) with Pakistan-based terror. It's a remarkable rise for a leader who joined mainstream BJP politics only in 2008 and is now among the top four ministers of the country. Whether it's the surgical strikes by the army and air force or the Rafale jets controversy, Nirmala Sitharaman is at the frontline of India's defence strategy and this government's political defence.**

* Interview conducted on 9 March 2019, New Delhi

The defence minister's office, where even the overarching sandstone corridors of South Block are imbued with a sense of history, is where decisions of war and peace have been taken. Its current occupant, fifty-nine-year-old Nirmala Sitharaman, dressed in a well-draped sari, is seated straight-backed behind a towering desk, the Indian flag strategically taking pride of place in the large room. She is aware of the historical legacy she bears, as we both look at the board listing previous defence ministers from R. Venkataraman to George Fernandes and Pranab Mukherjee. Her poise also doesn't hide the fact that she knows she occupies a unique position—only one of a handful of woman defence ministers in the world and the only one in South Asia.

'How has India's strategic defence changed after the Balakot air strikes, marking the first time since the 1971 War that India has gone deep into Pakistani territory?' I ask her. 'Do you see this as a key defining moment for India?'

Measured in her response, as always, she says, 'I don't know if I want to call it a defining moment, but it has definitely reset the way with which India deals with its strategic independence. All these years, our approach was extremely calibrated in handling issues dealing with the strategic independence of India, that is even more pronounced now. In a multipolar world, with so many countries positioning themselves strongly, India has been strengthening its bilateral relations with many different countries, but we have ensured we keep our strategic independence at the core of every relationship. Now we have gone one step further to show that we are not going to be waiting forever to respond on terrorism-related matters.'

On 14 February 2019, a suicide bomber rammed his vehicle packed with explosives into a convoy of CRPF jawans, killing forty paramilitary soldiers in Pulwama, in Jammu and Kashmir. The attack for which the Jaish-e-Mohammed, a Pakistan-based terror organization, claimed responsibility was a red flag to India. 'Was this the turning point that made the Indian government decide that enough was enough?' I ask.

'Post-Pulwama, we waited ten days for Pakistan to take action against terror camps,' Nirmala Sitharaman tells me, 'and then the call was taken. It was a clear call—we were not attacking anyone; it was not a negative or military step, it was clear targeting of the nerve centre of terror in Balakot, about which we had credible intelligence before we took this decision. Our decision came after an accumulation of efforts largely post the Mumbai attacks of 26/11, to get Pakistan to act against terror originating from their soil. There were dossiers of evidence completed even by the previous governments and submitted to Pakistan. Our diplomats repeatedly raised the issue at the United Nations, asking why some agencies in Pakistan were not being listed under terror networks. And the institutional memory we had, that despite all these efforts by India, since 2008 and Mumbai, a Pulwama still happened.

'It was clearly a significant point in the antiterrorism narrative that India needed, to show the blatant abuse from the territory of Pakistan. So, despite all the years of accumulated efforts, bilaterally with Pakistan and at the UN and at other international forums, Pakistan did not show any credible intent to take action. We had often reached out to them, saying we want peace in the neighbourhood; if it's possible with everyone else, why don't you want to do it? There had been no positive response, and then Pulwama happened. So, this narrative was festering with Indian policymakers and people in the government. The responsibility for the Pulwama terror attack was also claimed by a group that was located in Pakistan, about which the previous government, as well as this one, had given evidence to

Pakistan, yet no action was taken and now they've killed forty young men fighting for this country.

'More importantly,' she continues, 'there was palpable anger amongst the people, saying is this what we are going to live with, why are we not making Pakistan take necessary action?

'And now,' Nirmala Sitharaman says, 'I have an argument I would like to pose. After giving credible evidence and presenting dossiers, we needed to tell them [Pakistan] that we would wait up to a point. We were not going to sit back and watch them do nothing against terror. With the benefit of hindsight, I want to ask—would there have been such a major terror attack again had we taken a deterrent or punitive step after 26/11? Is it also a corollary for us to think that we didn't take substantive action back then and therefore, terror attacks kept happening? These are only questions; I can't answer them. No one can answer them because we are trying to predict the mind of someone in Pakistan, whether it is the establishment, the military, or the ISI. Although, I think if we had taken substantive action after 26/11, terrorism probably would not have been so blatant today,' she says.

The fact, however, remains that after every terror attack, there has been the larger question of nuclear escalation which is at the core of determining the response from India and the global community response. 'How far can things escalate between two nuclear nations? What happens now if another terror attack takes place?' I ask.

The defence minister responds immediately. 'On 26 February, what India did post-Pulwama was neither for war nor military action. It was a clearly targeted attack on terrorism. Both the previous and current government has repeatedly told Pakistan that they are hosting terror centers, training terrorists on their soil. It's not a surprise to Pakistan, or the globe, that they are hosting terrorists. Even the ceasefire violations that happen across the Indo-Pak border and the LoC through non-state actors happen with active support of their military. The terror attacks happen with the active support of the military there and we have evidence of this, telltale signs of who supplies the terror groups with material. This has been happening for the last twenty to thirty years. India can provide evidence for each ceasefire violation, for each terror attack on how the establishment in Pakistan is absolutely hand in glove with the terrorists. So, 26 February was more a surgical attack on a terrorist-training centre, for which we had credible intelligence inputs that more suicide bombers were being trained to carry out more Pulwama-like attacks in India.

'Our fighter jets went precisely to the location of the terror centre, finished it and came back. In fact, this was followed by Pakistan's military action, they came and and bombed our front posts, our military centres. We had not even touched their military networks or their civilian centres. We had clearly focused on one of their terrorist camps. How can both actions be equated?

'When people ask us if we should not be de-escalating the matter, I tell them that I have not escalated things in the first place. War is what happens when we attack them and they do the same as per certain established institutional frameworks. But, in this case, they're constantly attacking us like guerrilla warfare with non-state actors.'

'Another important strategic aspect that has emerged,' I point out, 'is the global response to India's strikes at Balakot. The de-hyphenation in the way the world looks at India and Pakistan now seems complete. Even China, a crucial ally for Pakistan, condemned the terror attacks in India.'

'The prime minister and the external affairs minister have been building on one thing very clearly and that is isolating Pakistan in the global community as the nerve centre and fountainhead for terrorism. We have repeatedly shown how several global money trails lead to terror networks in Pakistan, and that is why the global community stood by us post-Pulwama. I am not gloating about it,' says Nirmala. 'People have been able to see through the crocodile tears that Pakistan often sheds about being victims of terror. If they are victims of terror but also giving fodder and shelter to terrorist groups, what action are you taking?'

'Has Pulwama and its aftermath been the most difficult time for you in your two and half years as defence minister?' I ask.

'Pulwama is an incident which shook the conscience of every Indian, not just me,' she replies sombrely. 'I don't know how to describe the moment when I received the bodies of forty martyrs at the Delhi airport and waited for the prime minister and leaders from all the political parties to come and pay their respects. It cannot be described in words, Sonia, it just makes you feel hollow inside. Revulsion sets in when you think about the minds and hearts of the perpetrators behind these attacks . . .'

Nirmala Sitharaman also dismisses all reports that as defence minister, she was a token presence and not a core member of the inner team led by the prime minister, which was aware of India's air-strike response.

'These are very odd statements that come from the media every time. Were the ministers kept informed? I can only say that I have been in the complete picture from the very beginning. I was completely in the know of things and participated with everyone concerned.'

It wasn't just the prime minister who had a sleepless night during the operations, as he'd mentioned at an election rally. The IAF planes took off from India on the early morning of the 26th, hit the target at 3.30 a.m., and were all back safely in Indian airspace soon after.

The defence minister smiles as she says, 'On the 26th morning, when I received the call at 4 a.m., informing me that everyone was safe and all the pilots have come back, I heaved a sigh of relief. It was the other extreme of the emotion I felt after the Pulwama attack. When Wing Commander Abhinandan was captured a day later, I had monitored it very closely with the Indian High Commissioner to Pakistan, who was in Delhi for consultations, the Foreign Secretary, the Defence Secretary, and the three forces. The Cabinet Committee on Security was meeting, subsequently the national security council, so we were monitoring the situation nonstop and trying every measure we could to get him back safely. On the day of his return, there was intense coordination, there were certain ups and downs in the inputs that were coming in. But when he finally walked across the Wagah border, there was a great sense of relief. And when I met him the next day, it was very positive and motivating. I was very inspired by the Wing Commander, especially to see him keeping his spirits so high. He is an exemplary officer.'

Today, Nirmala Sitharaman is focused on the challenges of the immediate aftermath of India's strikes but much of her tenure has also been taken up with the political defence of what the Opposition regards as a corrupt aircraft deal—the purchase of thirty-six Rafale aircraft manufactured by Dassault in France. Though the deal was signed before she was defence minister, her combative replies in Parliament, press conferences in different cities and her visit to the aircraft manufacturers in Paris make Nirmala Sitharaman the government's front-line defence in the Rafale matter. 'Is this the Modi government's Bofors moment?' I ask, referring to the time when the Rajiv Gandhi government was hit with a corruption scandal in the purchase of Bofors guns from Sweden.

'Not at all,' she shoots back. 'My job is a cut-and-dried exercise of simply stating the facts. Stating the facts repeatedly and stating only the facts. I don't think it is a job that is very complicated, except that, it has to be done over and over again. Because facts don't seem to be understood by the Opposition that seems to revel in perpetrating falsehoods. So, it's my job to ensure that I don't get tired of telling the facts.

'I remind myself of the importance of a sensitive ministry,' she continues. 'Issues which have very serious and larger implications for national security need to be dealt with extreme caution. I tell myself to be absolutely contained and to be sure that I reveal only that information which is necessary to quell a campaign which is not based on facts. Containment is a necessary part of this job. National interest is the primary goal, not the desire to put down your opponent even for argument's sake.'

The word 'containment' seems to sum up Nirmala's essence too. Her poise never falters, her words are measured and articulate—a skill she's cultivated from her experience as a BJP spokesperson since she began appearing on TV in 2009. Her meteoric rise began then and her steely aggression on TV debates earned her a ministerial berth in 2014.

'Immediately after UPA-2's win in 2009, the BJP seemed to have settled into permanent opposition mode,' I point out, 'until the arrival of then Gujarat chief minister Narendra Modi and Amit Shah on the national stage. As an insider in BJP politics, when did you feel the mood had shifted to your moment, the Modi moment?'

'In 2010 and 2011, the BJP was doing rigorous work as an opposition party but hope started flickering in mid-2012. I felt that we could give a decent fight, we had a coherent narrative. But it was in September 2013 that I felt a momentous change when then chief minister Narendra Modi was declared the BJP's prime ministerial candidate.

'In fact,' she says, 'I'd see the "Modi era" as the defining moment in contemporary Indian politics. The mandate, this government coming into place—and what I strongly believe are very determined and defining decisions that have been made after the 2014 elections— has brought a fundamental change in India. We are witnessing the impact of all of it today.'

'What do you associate with this new Modi era?' I ask.

'Actual changes for social empowerment are happening now,' she answers emphatically, an impassioned spokesperson now for her coinage of this term. 'Why do I say that? Firstly, it's because for every decision which empowers the scheduled castes, legislative and legal steps are unfailingly being taken to ensure it is within the enshrinement of the Constitution. From economic well-being to administrative reform, social empowerment has been repeatedly reinforced. Secondly, there have been larger reforms to the system, like the anti-bankruptcy law, whether they are glamorous or not, certain cutting-edge changes, which are impacting the underbelly of the Indian political economy. These changes do not get votes but we still make them because deadwood needs to be removed and the undergrowth has to be cleared. Also, the prime minister has made India a global power in a way that's never been done before. His biggest achievement is in the international community through the global leaders isolating Pakistan. There's a saying: "We can change our friends but we can't change our neighbours."

'But only time will tell the full picture. It is hard for us to gauge the full extent of the reforms because we are in the moment. The true story and the complete narrative are going to be set only by history and therefore, I am grateful to God that I am an inside witness,' she says passionately.

Despite her articulate advocacy of the Modi doctrine, there are other aspects, not all of them benign, to this. One of them is a toxic cocktail of religion in our politics.

'When you talk about social change under the Modi government, do you think religion is a big part of politics today? Secularism seems to have been replaced by an overt display of Hinduism.'

'Religion has always been a part of our politics,' she responds quickly. 'The BJP or its workers are not saying that we must feel proud to be Hindu. That's not part of any strategy. But it's also something we cannot ignore. Secularism is a word which was overused. We will not ignore the minorities but not at the cost of the majority,' she says firmly.

A passionate advocacy of a doctrine which has come to represent the new reality of Indian politics today. However, shifting focus from the politics to the personal, I ask her about her remarkable rise along with the BJP and Modi, all the more striking because she had nothing to do with politics just over a decade ago.

'You had worked at PwC and then with the BBC in the late 1980s when you were in the United Kingdom with your husband [her husband, Dr Parakala Prabhakar, was media adviser to the Andhra Pradesh government and earlier with actor Chiranjeevi's party]. How did you get into politics?'

She breaks into a rare smile. 'I do have to give credit to the fact that the BJP chose to have 33 per cent reservation for women. In 2008, this decision was implemented whereby at every stage, from the panchayat to the national level, 33 per cent party posts had to be reserved for women and for someone who always believed in merit rather than gender, I must thank the party for calling and then choosing me. I was exposed to politics in 2003 when I had been a member of the National Commission for Women. It was only in 2008 when I became a member of the National Executive when Rajnath Singh was President.'

'But why did you join the BJP, especially since your husband's family was traditionally pro-Congress?'

'I'm married into a very political family. My husband's side of the family come from many different parties, so my exposure was wide. However, when the opportunity came in 2008, it was my mother-in-law who I'd credit for my decision. She was a Congress MLA and told me that, one way or the other, it was important to contribute to the country. How did it matter which party one belonged to? I believed in many of the ideologies the BJP party stands for—making India its priority, looking at India as a whole. Many of these goals resonated with me. And, so, I took a leap of faith.'

'Was it a difficult journey?' I ask.

'To be honest, I haven't had half the problems that many other women in politics have faced,' she admits. 'However, I think it takes much more power from a woman to be at par with a man. The BJP does not hesitate to bring in efficient and skilled people from different backgrounds, it gives them a chance to grow in the party. The image of the "patriarchal" BJP is actually incorrect. No other party, not even the Communist party, has the divergence of women from different backgrounds that we do.'

Facts do bear that out. The Modi government today has more women ministers in powerful positions than ever before, and almost none of them are from political families. 'You went from a first-time member of Parliament to a minister of independent charge to Cabinet minister and then defence minister in just two years; how did you handle this meteoric rise?'

'Well, looking back, it's been nearly two and a half years here and when I drive up Raisina Hill, I just look up at the majestic structure and think, is this actually my office? I hope I can live up to my predecessors.

'On 3 September 2016, the day of the swearing-in ceremony at Rashtrapati Bhavan, I still didn't know what my new portfolio would be. When I was at home talking to the media, Arun Jaitley called, asking me to meet him immediately. I went to his residence and then, the Cabinet Secretary called me, telling me that he was at my home. It was then that Mr Jaitley informed me that I was going to be the defence minister. My daughter, who was going abroad for her studies, had postponed her trip for a day for the reshuffle. She came for the swearing-in and then went to Khan Market. When she saw the news on TV, she was furious that I hadn't told her. But she was so excited that she forgave me.' Nirmala smiles.

In her tenure so far, Nirmala Sitharaman hasn't spent much time at the Raisina Hill office as she's constantly on tours to remote outposts of the armed forces and with political campaigns. From Siachen to flying on a Sukhoi, one of the IAF's most powerful fighter jets, she is a defence minister who believes in first-hand experiences.

'Visiting the Siachen Glacier and the troops there was one thing, but there are some posts which are possibly as bad as or worse than Siachen, and I chose to go to those places. These trips were a revelation. One of the posts near the Tibet border is so remote that they don't even have proper tracks. After a certain point, even mules don't go any further. Look at the environment they work in. I had broken protocol and asked the troops about their problems. They didn't lose their composure at all. They asked me not to worry about them, that they were there to guard the borders. Of course, there were small things they needed, like cell-phone service to talk to their families. But they never asked me the core question—why are we serving in such remote areas—or doubted their presence there. Never!' she says passionately. 'These are soldiers from all over India. These things got me thinking and I've made it a point to go to those camps where no raksha mantri [defence minister] has gone before.'

One thing Ms Sitharaman doesn't like is her gender being her calling card. Yet, the symbolism is evident along with the substance.

'Indira Gandhi was your female predecessor at this post. She was called "Ma Durga" after what happened in the 1971 war where India defeated Pakistan and the creation of Bangladesh. Do you see any similarities between her and you?'

'However tempting it might be, I do not want to compare myself to Mrs Gandhi. She was the prime minister and the insurgencies during her time, particularly, leading to the Indo-Pakistan War of 1971, were events unique to a certain period of history and a certain leadership which prevailed then. So, I would never compare myself with her, just because she is a woman,' she responds.

'But, yes, the way the defence ministry has played its role, and we both, Sonia, keep referring to the list behind me [a wooden plaque that bears the name of every defence minister since Independence etched in gold letters]; the criticality of this ministry, it's important role, constantly plays in my head. And because it does so, I can make sure that I go back to say—Yes, I have done what is right today. I have benefited by the advice given and at the same time, I have kept everybody informed—those who must know—almost on a daily basis. So, my greatest achievement, and that's what I strive to do better every day, is to play my role consciously. Live every minute that I am here, consciously, and perform the role I am expected to, so that I can honour those who have come before me. Only then will I be able to say that I have done justice to the job.'

'Finally,' I ask, 'where do you see your role in history, Ms Sitharaman?'

She smiles as she answers, 'As a cog in a big wheel, forever moving like the wheel of Jagannath. A cog in the process of keeping this country safe.'

Whether it be the wheel of Jagannath or the Modi juggernaut, Nirmala Sitharaman is now an integral part of a larger Modi era in Indian politics, foreign policy, and security strategy. Her perspective is unique because she is at its epicentre. But as she says, the Modi government's and her contribution to India's transformation is something that will be judged by tomorrow's historians.

[5]

Amartya Sen

The Shaping of a Nobel Laureate

He's eighty-five and visibly frail now, but Nobel Laureate, Professor Amartya Sen remains an intellectual giant. Even though he's been conferred a Bharat Ratna and is currently the best-known welfare economist in the world, the lifetime Harvard professor is also a red flag to the Modi government and has been summarily dismissed from anything to do with public policy. Yet, Professor Sen, who has kept his Indian citizenship and spends a few months in Shantiniketan, West Bengal, every year, remains passionately engaged with India.*

* Interview conducted on 17 August 2018, New Delhi

Amartya Sen has written evocatively of witnessing the human devastation caused by the Bengal famine of 1943 and its influence on his work. What is less well known, however, is what he sees as the defining moments he has witnessed that have impacted contemporary India.

'Many things have happened in the last seventy-five-odd years, including terrible things like the Bengal famine. Obviously, I have very clear memories of that and the sudden eruption of Hindu–Muslim communal riots in the 1940s. Then again, there were great and positive things happening like Independence and the Indian Constitution and the stability of the democratic system, including the defeat of the Emergency.

'However,' he continues, 'if you pressed me with a gun about what was most consequential, taking into account what is happening to India today, I would probably say the particular incident of seeing someone who had been just knifed by communal thugs. Qadir Miya stumbled into our compound in Dhaka, when I was eleven, profusely bleeding and wanting help—he couldn't be saved.'

Sixty-five years later, the traumatic incident is still fresh in Professor Sen's mind. He describes the context in vivid detail.

'The riots were just beginning in 1944. Bengal didn't have many riots until the 1940s. The first electoral victory of the Muslim League in Bengal was only in 1946; all the earlier elections were won by secular parties like the Congress or the peasant parties. It was a newly cultivated communal situation in which riots were suddenly erupting. There was a daily wage labourer called Qadir Miya who needed some income because his family was starving. So at a huge risk, he accepted the offer of a day's job in the Wari area in Dhaka,

which is mainly a Hindu area, where we lived. He was knifed by a
violent Hindu mob on the street outside our home. He staggered
into our garden and he was lying on my lap, bleeding, and I was
shouting, and my father emerged and immediately took him to the
hospital. He died there.'

The calmness with which he describes a man bleeding to death
in his lap when he was just eleven accentuates the horror of the
crime.

'The incident had a devastating impact on me,' he says. 'Firstly,
I had never seen a murder before. Secondly, I couldn't understand
why somebody would try to kill this man when he had done no
harm. Indeed, the killer didn't even know who this man was. The
murderer knew that the victim was a Muslim but that's all. I found
it very difficult to understand. Several things hit me but one of them
was the fact that you could be barbarously violent and murderously
determined to eliminate someone on the grounds of fighting what
you take to be an enemy group with a different identity from yours—
in this case a Muslim. Similar things were happening in the Muslim
areas where Hindus were being killed, so there was no asymmetry
in that. Another big symmetry was that the easiest people to kill in
this kind of violence, of course, were the poorest people who didn't
have secure homes and because of their work had to go out. That
made them vulnerable. The wealthier Muslims and wealthier Hindus
were not vulnerable in the way the poor were of both communities.
So, even though the murder was because of the Hindu–Muslim
divide, the victimhood made a distinction between the poor and the
vulnerable on one side and the relatively better protected and safe on
the other side.'

'Do you think then poverty almost overrules identity when it
comes to clashes like these?' I ask him.

'You see, if you think about Qadir Miya's identity, there's his
Muslim identity, which is why he got killed by these Hindu thugs.
He also had an identity as a labourer, as a poor person, and because

of that he took the risk of going into a hostile area for a tiny reward. If he didn't have to do manual work at a subsistence wage to earn a little income, he wouldn't have had to take the risk. One of the things Qadir told me as he lay on my lap and my father was getting the car out was that he had gone out because his children were hungry and he needed some money to feed them. His wife had told him, "Don't go, don't take the risk, that's a Hindu area, you would be in great danger." He told me, "She was right, but I had to violate her advice because I looked at my children and I had to get some them food, so I went out." So that's another identity which forced him into this vulnerable situation, an identity as a poor person, a labourer with a very low wage, with dependent children. So, he had multiple identities, but it also made me think that if you don't have economic freedom, not being able to survive through a crisis without having to take awful risks, you could be in great difficulty. Here, lack of economic freedom actually endangers your freedom to survive.'

A big part of Amartya Sen's body of work examines concepts like these and as he narrates this incident, I get a sense of how deeply his childhood experiences have shaped the Nobel Laureate.

'My early experiences influenced both my concerns with inequality (including inequality as a cause of deprivation and death), as well as identity-based, well-organized bias which killed Qadir Miya (and which killed so many hundreds of thousands of other people). They came face-to-face with me very early in my life,' he said.

Professor Sen points out the chilling lack of fear of consequences that are characteristics of anarchy.

'My father described to the police the people who had murdered Qadir Miya,' he remembers. 'The thugs were quite well known in the area and my father thought that he could help to identify which group it was. So he went to the police station and they just said they weren't interested.'

There are linkages Professor Sen wants to draw between those old events and what he thinks is happening in today's India.

'I think it's all parallel to what is going on right now. Like people being identified as being Muslims (or Dalits) and being connected with either beef-eating or doing something else like cow stealing, that must be stopped. These are essentially identity issues in 2019, like the murder in 1944 was an identity murder. This was a Muslim person and the thugs who killed Qadir Miya didn't know anything about him other than the fact that he was Muslim. This has to be distinguished by the way from a different kind of identity murder—from a behaviour-oriented murder of a person, whose behaviour is something to which others take severe, narrow-minded objection like Gauri Lankesh, the outspoken journalist, or M.M. Kalaburgi the rationalist; you identify something of theirs you don't like and you kill them for it. The other kind is when you identify a person belonging to a community—it doesn't matter what they're doing—you kill them for just belonging to a particular community; that silent identity is enough reason there.

'The third element that was interesting for me is: how come the police didn't have any interest in the crime when they knew about it? Think of Rakbar Khan—he was killed near Alwar in 2018 on the mere suspicion of cow smuggling. If you think about it, he did not have a particular view like Gauri Lankesh or Kalaburgi; he was killed because he was identified as belonging to a group, the difference between the identification of being a Muslim and being a beef eater or handler is little because of their communal identification—which is why this person was maltreated and lynched. There have been many other cases over the last few months. If you look at the last couple of years, the majority of the violent killing cases by religious goons have been related to cows.'

Amartya Sen has worked on many complex problems of social choice theory (his Nobel Prize relates to them), but in the context of present-day India, violence related to vocal identity (like being an outspoken rationalist) or silent identity (for example, in the name of protecting the cow), is something Professor Sen finds astonishing and appalling. 'Are we at a turning point in Indian democracy, rather than going forward? Are we at a churning point where we need to introspect?' I ask.

'It's a turning point in the sense that India has not been so narrow-minded in this respect for a long time, perhaps ever before. Even at the time of the riots, there was some shame about the riots—I am thinking of the pre-Partition riots, in Bengal, Punjab, Delhi. There was also a sense of "this is wrong", which is why when Mahatma Gandhi stood firmly, as he did, there was an immediate response. What has happened now is a kind of legitimization of this idea that cows are holy, and we ought to protect them. As it happens, most Hindus have been traditionally offended in being described only in terms of the "holy cow", but now there seems to be great pride in an alleged religious intimacy with the cow—giving it priority. In the case of Rakbar, they made sure the cows were safely sent to the shelter before the person who was attacked and wounded was taken to the hospital. It's no longer a situation where Hindus take pride in the Upanishads and the Gita; that doesn't interest the activist as much as some apparently foundational rules: "we revere cows", "we don't eat them", "nasty people eat them", "nasty people do business with their skin". This kind of thinking seems to have become the dominant image of Hinduism in terms of action, which it wasn't until fairly recently. So, there has been a change and yet, what it has exploited is of course a sense of confused anger, that may or may not be present in many societies (it has been present in India quite a lot of the time), but which can be separated out and made into a weapon of violence through engineered prominence. It's a question of making terrifying use of the confusion in treating others violently.

'Perhaps earlier there was more internal doubt about the legitimacy of the confused anger, and about the case for using it to be violent to others. However, right now the groups that have been very active in these lynchings (and other violent activities) don't seem to have any doubt in their mind. Secondly, there have always been

people, Mahatma Gandhi, Rabindranath Tagore, and others who
have stood against such violence. Today, it's obviously hard to find a
parallel to Mahatma Gandhi but not even a distant image of him can
be easily found either. Also, at this time, the ruling government itself
is inclined to take clearly a partisan view, as they seem to be doing.'

Interestingly, Amartya Sen has often been pitched as an opponent
of the government's pro-capitalist reforms (including premature
privatization of social services), and he has used his Nobel Prize money
to set up trusts to advance public health and school education in India
and Bangladesh. However, as he speaks passionately, it's clear that
he is just as worried about what he sees as an assault on minorities.
He is aware of the historical connection with the inheritance of
British rule—when Hindus felt persecuted in their own land—which
contributed to a fundamental change in the nature of Hindu thinking.

'In the imperial context in India, Hindus were often thought
to be lowly creatures, and the British—certainly mid-nineteenth
century onwards—regarded Indians to be pretty lowly creatures as
well. Winston Churchill declared that the Indians are the "beastliest
people in the world, along with the Germans". Within that, there
was a particular non-admiration, if I may put it like that, for the
Hindus. So, I can see that in that biased context people would want
to fight that slanted perception. Now there's one way of fighting
which Vivekananda did—he said, well, that's not what we stand
for, *this* is what we stand for and we try not to get angry and go
around hitting others in defence of our own religion. Many proud
Hindus of that period had strong convictions on this.

'However, when you think about the contemporary Hindutva
movement, even though people can still criticize the narrowness of
the sectarian vision, as Tagore and Gandhi had done in the past,
there is something new here today. The idea that we could defend
ourselves, or our religion, by lynching Muslims or Dalits—that is a
different story altogether—with a new focus. Along with that change
also comes the concoction of history that the Mughals didn't win

the victories, all the victories were won by the Hindu kings like
Rana Pratap. "We won, but somehow the Pathans and the Mughals
came to rule the country."' He pauses as he chuckles. 'There's a
mysterious story there but that story is widely advocated (even in
school textbooks) and repeated again and again.'

'As this idea of "correcting" our history is such a flashpoint in
today's India, what are the moments that have been turning points
in India's history?' I ask.

'We have gone through terrible famines, terrible natural disasters
and yet the people have stood there and fought it,' he replies. 'They
have come out unbroken. Now, that is true of common labour, that
is true of very exploited factory workers, very maltreated domestic
servants and so on. They have found a way of taking the world as
it is and still not become murderously nasty. The nastiness we see
around us has not been spontaneous, it has been generated; organized
through propaganda and preaching. No Hindu–Muslim riot almost
without exception has started in the rural areas, they are typically
urban phenomena. They're largely fed into rural areas from outside.
The common people have typically resisted the mistreatment of
others, and in this India has something to be proud of.

'Unfortunately, that doesn't prevent the possibility of exciting
people to do nasty things, as indeed many of these communal youths
do when they are instigated and encouraged to go after Dalits or
Muslims. Even then the evil propaganda does not typically get the
support of a majority. People, despite the fact that the winds have
been flowing in the contrary direction, have shown a great deal of
resistance and courage. Indeed, sometimes much more—with social
sympathy and independence. Fearless students have agitated even
when they have been accused of sedition in a way that is almost
certainly not legally acceptable. Even when they've been arrested,
beaten in custody, physically attacked while on trial—the student
leaders have stood their ground. There is a lot to admire in such
courage and dedication. We admire them but we also admire the

population at large who have offered resistance to political plans of single-community dominance.'

Professor Sen goes on to elucidate that the majority of Indians have never supported 'majoritarian rule'—silencing the voices of minorities.

'At the moment, the narrow-minded sectarian governance that we tend to think of as "Hindutva rule" does not have anywhere near the support of a Hindu majority. Modi's BJP got a majority of seats in the parliament with only 31 per cent of the vote. India has more than 80 per cent Hindus, and yet, never have the narrow-minded sectarian Hindu politics had majority support. It is a mistake to call them "majoritarian Hindu". The majority of Hindus have never voted for Hindutva,' the Nobel Laureate points out.

'Do you feel this is just a phase in our turbulent history?' I ask.

'I don't think one can just say that. That's an argument for sitting tight and hoping that the storm will pass. It is a storm that we can confront. It won't pass on its own so if there is one thing that the Indian tradition has taught us again and again is that there is ultimately nothing more important than reasoning. Whether you're looking in the Rig Veda or in the Upanishads, Krishna and Arjun in the Gita, or Akbar's pronouncements, they are believers in reason. And we must remember the biggest name of all—Buddha—who invariably stands up for reason. I think it's through reason that we have to win the battle.

'When I arrived at Trinity College as an undergraduate in 1953, on the first day, I went to see the chapel. I couldn't believe the number of names of fallen Trinity men in the First World War I found. I could hardly stand—I was so upset to see how many people were killed in the First World War. All the walls of the chapel filled with their names. So many people from just one college, one age group, were killed in a European war that lasted only four years. Now that seems like an unbelievable story—and surely, it's now gone in Europe. What changed? What changed is the reasoning about the silliness of European wars.

'I think that's what we have to fight—the narrow-mindedness and inanity of taking a deliberately divisive view of India, which doesn't do India any good, nor does it give any glorious service to Hinduism. The propaganda for a concocted view of a "Hindu India" doesn't have the numbers, but it can cause a lot of terror through powerful political organization. It doesn't have sound reasoning, but it can have deceptive reason that at least influences a lot of people ready to run with a sectarian programme. Ultimately, we have to fight with reason, with our pride in humanity.

'If we come back to Qadir Miya, in 1944, when the communal riots were going on, I asked my parents why this man got killed, lying on my lap, bleeding profusely—it looked as if this would never end. But within eight years of that, the riots were all gone. People in Bengal—including what would become Bangladesh—began agitating about the Bengali language and culture instead. It did not change automatically. It changed because there were leaders who were asking for it with reason and people were beginning to agitate for a real change,' he says emphatically, giving us a rare perspective from 1944 to 2019.

It's been a fascinating conversation following the threads over seven decades and the threads of the distant past that still bind us today. 'Finally, Professor Sen,' I ask, 'are you optimistic about the India of the future?'

'I am always optimistic,' he says with a laugh. 'I had cancer when I was eighteen and I was told I had a 15 per cent chance of living at the most for five years. That was sixty-five years ago. At the moment, I am fighting an aggressive form of cancer of the prostate and I hope to win over it. At least I am trying to do what I can to win, rather than just giving up. I am optimistic because I believe in humanity, the ability to tell good from bad, to reason about what we want, and to reason about what, if anything, we can do about our problems.'

Professor Amartya Sen has fought injustice from the age of eleven to eighty-five, and even now, a lion in winter, he remains the government's most formidable intellectual opponent.

[6]

Raghuram Rajan

The Rajan Effect

Former chief economist at the International Monetary Fund (IMF), former chief economic adviser (CEA) to Prime Minister Manmohan Singh, former Reserve Bank of India (RBI) Governor, and now distinguished services professor at the business school at the University of Chicago, Raghuram Rajan has made a habit of collecting accolades including being named in a list of possible future Nobel Prize winners.* And he's only fifty-five years old. Yet, this is the man the Modi government chose not to give a second term to for RBI Governor and who faced constant criticism from the RSS and other right-wing economic thinkers during his tenure. This hasn't deterred Rajan from remaining closely connected to India. He recently released 'An Economic Strategy for India'†—a five-year economic plan for governments, along with twelve other economists like Gita Gopinath, Abhijit Banerjee, Amartya Lahiri.‡

---

* https://www.ndtv.com/india-news/raghuram-rajan-among-probables-for-nobel-prize-for-economics-reports-1759985

† https://www.bloombergquint.com/global-economics/an-economic-strategy-for-india-by-rajan-gopinath-and-others-full-report#gs.8vJgH6kQ

‡ Interview conducted on 3 December 2018 when Dr Rajan was in Chicago

Raghuram Rajan first made international headlines when he famously predicted the global recession in 2005, three years before it happened. 'How did your India story begin and what, according to you, were the key defining moments, both from your perspective first as CEA and then as RBI Governor?' I ask him.

'I want to set this moment in the context of India's development and the moment I'd like to talk about is the currency turmoil we experienced in 2013 when the Indian rupee had fallen by as much as 20 per cent to the dollar at one stage after the taper tantrum. The reason I want to set the context,' Rajan continues, 'is that, in my mind, it created the impetus for moving ahead on one of our major economic institutions today, which is the inflation-targeting framework and the Monetary Policy Committee. This may seem small in the larger scheme of things, but I think it reflects institutional development and, of course, in India we develop institution in lurches; for every two steps forward, we sometimes take one back. Demonetization was a step back, but hopefully over the longer run we will create the structures we need to become a modern economy,' he says.

However, before we explore that in greater detail, what is interesting is the timing of Raghuram Rajan's decision to return to India. After his stint as IMF chief economist in Washington, in 2012 he came to a volatile Indian political economy to face a series of challenges as CEA to then prime minister Manmohan Singh.

'When I finished at the IMF as chief economist, Prime Minister Manmohan Singh asked me to take a look at the Indian financial sector,' Raghuram Rajan explains. 'We had published a report on the reforms required to place the sector on a stable footing. In that process, I had developed a rapport with the prime minister. At the time, things were going from bad to worse in India. After the global crisis, inflation was picking up, the current account deficit and fiscal deficit were widening. It was in the summer of 2012 when Mr Chidambaram came back to the finance ministry. I had known Mr Chidambaram as finance minister from my days at the IMF. At that point, I received a call from Dr C. Rangarajan [former RBI Governor and chairman of the prime minister's Economic Advisory Council] asking me if I was interested in doing something here. I had to face the question that at some point every Indian faces— how much are you prepared to contribute to national service? One can talk the talk, but eventually, one has to stop complaining and actually do something,' says Dr Rajan. 'Of course, it was a difficult time in India economically speaking.' He then adds, laughing, 'On the other hand, what better time for an economist to step up when there's a need for change and possibility of change?'

Interestingly, I point out, much of the flak the government got back then was about how an economist-turned-prime-minister had allowed the economy to fall into a shambles.

'Yes,' says Dr Rajan. 'The prime minister was getting a tremendous amount of flak but it's important to understand that at the same time he was willing to absorb it and perhaps react in the right way. I was on a panel, in 2012, with T.N. Ninan and Isher Ahluwalia, talking about how the economy had eroded since the 2007–08 high point of growth and we were complaining about the drift. The fourth person sitting on the dais was Dr Manmohan Singh. He had listened to us talk and then told us that he would need to reflect on the matter if everyone was talking about it. He was willing to accept criticism provided it was constructive. I think that's because he was going to start the process of fiscal consolidation which Mr Chidambaram then laid out later in 2012. If we hadn't started that process back then, India could have been in a much more severe crisis when things turned in the global economy a year later.

There is an American saying—if you can't stand the heat don't get in the kitchen. And that is really the point about public policy. You will face criticism, but do you think you can make a difference?'

Educated at India's top institutes—the Indian Institute of Technology, Delhi and then the Indian Institute of Management, Ahmedabad—Raghuram Rajan completed his PhD from the Massachusetts Institute of Technology (MIT) and had never worked in the Indian government. Walking into the finance ministry at North Block for the first time wasn't entirely what he expected.

'Well . . .' he laughs, 'coming into the finance ministry for the first time is, firstly, a culture shock! People stand up when one walks into a room—sometimes you have to do it, at other times, others do it to you. It's a culture I wasn't used to. That sense of deference doesn't typically exist in other places outside bureaucracy. Second, we were still working with files! Thick files in the day of electronics and computers! We still had to write in the margins. Even those in India who move from the private sector to the government will find it different. More importantly, in the private sector, if you decide to do something, it's usually done. In my first week at the ministry, there was the issue of rising grain prices, and the government had enormous buffer stocks of grain. I was in charge of a committee, to take a decision regarding this matter. The solution was obvious—we had to release the excess grain into the market to reduce its price. I felt so good after the decision was taken. I thought we'd achieved something; that we'd actually helped use the buffer stock to reduce prices for the public. However, I soon realized that the committee decision meant nothing. The issue went into some kind of black hole and many months later, I was still trying to figure out why we hadn't sold the excess grain,' he says.

'The bureaucracy is a black hole and many worthwhile projects get absorbed into it unless you keep pushing. And even if you have all the backing in the world, things don't get done,' he says. 'At the same time, if you have access to the key players who have a mandate, then there is a possibility of making a difference. For example, in Mr Chidambaram's budget in 2013, there was the need to simultaneously bring down the deficit and also spur growth. He was looking for ideas for how to do this. We finally came up with a sort of an investment tax benefit—if you invest you get a tax credit. This strategy required doing, it required thinking and it was announced in the budget. It's things like this that make you feel that, perhaps, I've made a small difference.'

The state of the economy at the time didn't make Dr Rajan and the government's task any easier. In 2013, India's current account deficit had started expanding because people started buying gold.

'Part of the reason people were buying gold is because inflation was rising at a very high rate. They were buying gold to hedge against high inflation. So, when Ben Bernanke, head of the US Federal Reserve, announced that the fed was tightening or reducing its buying of bonds, India had pretty bad numbers. There was a large fiscal deficit, large trade deficit, large current account deficit, and high inflation. These bad macro numbers frighten foreign investors and make them leave. Every day, we saw billions of dollars in investments leaving India. Whatever intervention the RBI did was proving ineffective. The rupee plunged by 20 per cent. At the time, India was known as one of the "Fragile Five" and every analyst in India was competing with the other to put a higher number at where the rupee would get to before it stabilized. Some were even talking of a hundred to the dollar. It was a very difficult time and we knew that our import bill would go up tremendously if the rupee plunged because our oil was being purchased at the dollar rate. We were also subsiding oil considerably, so if the price of petroleum went up, so would our subsidies and our fiscal deficit. It was a vicious cycle. The RBI and finance ministry got together to discuss matters, but nothing seemed to be working,' he recounts.

It was a time of long days and little sleep for Raghuram Rajan as CEA, at a time when every government intervention was failing.

'Yes. In fact, someone saw me at an airport lounge in August 2013, and they told me that I looked older and wondered what had happened.' Rajan laughs. 'It was a strain. I was watching TV all the time, monitoring where the rupee is, trying to figure out what will work.[§] We needed to restore confidence and it simply wasn't happening. The markets were betting against us in a big way and we were losing. So, then I was asked to take over the RBI in 2013.'

As RBI Governor, Dr Rajan had no choice but to hit the ground running.

'Since we were going into elections, there would be constant political blockage by the Opposition to any kind of reforms. Therefore, we weren't going to get any big reform, like the Goods and Services Tax, which would energize or convince investors that India was economically stable in the long run. However, after the financial crisis, growth was picking up slowly. There were many reforms in the report I had written for the prime minister. So two or three weeks before I was to take over, I went to the RBI and started talking to people about what we could do—actions that would boost confidence, reforms we could propose, if we could offer an alternative narrative to what was happening in India so that people didn't just focus on the political gridlock and corruption scandals; shift the focus to the positive plans.

'We put together a plan to ensure that money came in. Essentially, we gave banks an effective guarantee on the foreign exchange rate they would be able to convert money they brought in back. If the rupee strengthened, we would make money on the deal, if it didn't, we would lose money. Our priority was confidence-building, therefore we finally decided to put our money behind this whole process.

[§] FT.com/lexicon

Also, there were many actual reforms—such as opening up licensing of banks and putting a time frame by which we would announce bank licences, creating electronic bill payment structures, freeing up branching—that were part of the package which I announced on my first day in office. Who knows what actually drives markets, but they seemed to rally after that, and even though we had an election approaching, things started turning around. The rupee certainly strengthened, and the possibility that the political gridlock would be broken encouraged investors to come in, so we had a fortuitous set of circumstances. Inflation also started decreasing because we had raised interest rates. In fact, we raised rates three times at a time the government was heading into elections,' he points out.

Raghuram Rajan faced two very different sets of challenges in his four years in India. First, as CEA to the ministry of finance and then transitioning over to the other side to become the RBI Governor in 2013. This time his focus was to protect the RBI's autonomy from the finance ministry. And in his avatar as RBI Governor, Dr Rajan certainly wasn't taking any orders from anyone. Interest rates had been a point of conflict between previous RBI Governor D. Subbarao and two Congress finance ministers—Pranab Mukherjee and P. Chidambaram.[*]

I ask him how the hiked interest rates played out between Mr Chidambaram and him because they are both very strong-headed individuals.

'Mr Chidambaram is both extremely intelligent and a very forceful personality so we had long "discussions" about this matter,' says Dr Rajan with a chuckle. 'But people don't realize that the structure between the finance ministry and the RBI is set up for this kind of

---

[*] In his book, *Who Moved my Interest Rate*, D. Subbarao writes of how he faced pressure from both ministers on lowering interest rates, leading to last-minute tension over his reappointment and the refusal to extend the term of two of his deputies.

friction because the RBI Governor is ultimately under the finance minister. It is the finance minister who appoints the Governor, but there are times when the Governor has to stand up to his boss. The right boss, and this has been true of many finance ministers, understands this logic and respects it, so the Governor knows that he can push to a certain degree. So, basically, it's the art of persuasion,' says Dr Rajan.

'Fortunately, I had to raise interest rates only in the UPA and I cut interest rates in the NDA time. [Governments usually prefer lower interest rates because it makes lending easier and brings liquidity to the economy. The Reserve Bank is more cautious on cutting rates because of its impact on inflation.] However, the experience made me realize that we need to depoliticize the whole process, and the way to do it was to create the inflation committee and the monetary policy committee. I'm glad we did that because it takes the constant back and forth on the level of interest rates away from one person to a committee which can make those decisions.

'It's interesting, you use the word "fortunately" when you say you cut interest rates under the Modi government. What was it like, as RBI Governor, dealing with a dramatic political transition and two very different prime ministers—Dr Manmohan Singh and Mr Modi?' I ask.

'You have to meet, you have to persuade, you have to bring people to your way of thinking as much as possible. They will have their own views and you must find out how to accommodate your views to theirs in a way which minimizes friction. There is a tremendous amount of behind-the-scenes work, which never gets out into the open. One of the interesting things in India is that ideas emerge at some point in time, they never get taken up then, but they slowly make their way through various people, some champions emerge and then they get taken up.'

However, an idea which Rajan didn't come around to was demonetization. At the time when the policy was announced, his term as the RBI Governor had ended only a few short months ago.

It was widely believed that had it happened while he was still in office, he would've never signed off on it. In fact, the government's decision not to extend his tenure may have been linked to his opposition when the idea was first presented to him as RBI Governor.

'It's very hard to speculate on what might have happened,' Dr Rajan responds. 'It's not clear what one would have done at that point and I don't want to stand up and say I would have tendered my resignation or not accepted it—you have to react to circumstances at that point. I do think it was a mistake and I had made that very clear well before it was announced. Even when I was Governor, I tried my best to persuade various constituencies not to go in that direction because I was afraid it would be a problem. Of course, as the RBI Governor and as part of the establishment, we had to prepare for it. We were half prepared when it was announced but we would not have been prepared at all if the RBI hadn't begun work on this,' he says.

'Did the prime minister ask you your views on demonetization?' I interject.

'I spoke with every level of the government; I don't want to go beyond that,' he replies. 'I thought there were better ways to achieve the same objectives. The point, however, is that it is very easy to say when you're not faced with an actual decision. It's unfair for me to make any statements now when I was not faced with the decision.'

In September, Rajan returned to business school in Chicago. Three months later demonetization was announced. What was his first reaction when he heard the prime minister's announcement of demonetization on 8 November 2016?

'We all remember where we were on that day,' he says. 'It was the day of the US elections and I recollect saying they could not possibly be prepared at this point of time.'

Ironically, while some economists have said that demonetization broke the backbone of the informal sector, politically it seemed to have paid off for the BJP government. As an observer of political economy, what is Raghuram Rajan's take?

'You have to look at the overall benefits and costs of any action.' He pauses and then continues, 'We have been waiting for the long-term benefits of demonetization and as of now, it's hard to say that either corruption has come down or tax revenues have gone up significantly. I'm happy to be corrected on both those points but it's hard for me to gauge that in the data. Similarly, on the political side, since the Uttar Pradesh elections were held soon after demonetization, it seemed to suggest that the BJP's resounding victory in those elections meant that demonetization did not impact people negatively. However, what it has done over time is essentially set back an incipient recovery of the Indian economy.

'Of course, slow growth was compounded by the initial travails of GST—which I think longer term was a very good idea—but we slowed down when the world economy was growing faster. People tend to look at India in a static sense. But 2017 was a wonderful year for the global economy. Europe was doing very well, China was not slowing so much, but we slowed considerably. In the longer run, the economic effects of demonetization have to be considered. It is perhaps partly responsible for the dissatisfaction we see with farmer unrest and the 25 million people applying for 90,000 railway jobs. You have to wonder how much a decision like demonetization, which was no doubt done over a short period of time, could force many informal businesses to shut down. When you look at the Centre for Monitoring the Indian Economy's [CMIE] report on jobs, it shows a sharp decline just around the period of demonetization,' he concludes in perhaps one of the most lucid explanations I've heard so far of the post-demonetization impact.

However, while demonetization may go down as the Modi's government's biggest economic blunder, the UPA government and Raghuram Rajan are facing political heat today for the issue of bad loans or non-performing assets (NPAs) on the balance sheets of public-sector banks. Non-performing assets today are estimated to be nearly Rs 9 lakh crores or almost 11 per cent of total bank loans with both the prime minister and the Congress trading charges over who is responsible for the current situation.' Raghuram Rajan, as then Governor of the RBI, had been asked by a parliamentary committee to submit an analysis of why the NPA crisis happened. His seventeen-page report includes the famous 'Rajan List' in which he revealed that he had submitted a list of 'high-profile' fraud cases of NPAs to the prime minister's office for coordinated investigation. The list was submitted in February 2015, but he has had no update on the investigation.

'One of the big concerns when I was RBI Governor was the bad debt that was building up in the banking system,' he says. 'There were two constraints to dealing with it—first, we had a process of forbearance (ignoring these bad loans) in the past. This is a point of contention between the RBI and every finance ministry. Every finance ministry doesn't want to declare these as NPAs because it will disrupt growth; new lending won't happen. So, they want the RBI to display forbearance and hope that the bad loans will go away, so that the economy will revive, and they won't have to do anything about it. It's like an ostrich sticking its head in the sand, hoping that everything will get better. Every finance ministry, including the current one, wants the RBI to do that. But obviously, when the time comes, they point to the RBI's previous forbearance, which, often, had not worked out, saying the RBI had been asleep at the wheel, so why not do it again! None of this need be ascribed to vested interests or corruption. The finance ministry's instinct is to hope and pray that these bad problems will go away without trying to tackle them on their watch.'

That certainly wasn't how Governor Rajan wanted to deal with it on his watch though.

'I was receiving reports that things were worse than they seemed. The private sector and our own supervisors reported that there was a sense of unease. The real problem was that once we force them all to declare these as NPAs and force them to come clean, then what? Respectable bankers in the public-sector system, whom I thought very highly of, were saying that the moment you declare this as an NPA, we're going to stop lending and once we stop lending, this is going to go kaput. I didn't want to break the system, but I did want to clean it up and ensure that while lending continued, we'd cleaned up some of these bad debts and prevented more good money flowing after bad. So, the first thing we did was to create a whole new set of structures—such as the Strategic Debt Restructuring [SDR] scheme—to help banks restructure. We worked with the finance ministry and with SEBI [Securities and Exchange Board of India] to make this happen. In the absence of an actual bankruptcy code, this was about as much as we could do to create ways for the banks to recover. Having created these structures, we now forced banks to come clean by ensuring they treated loans by the book. If, in fact, they were tempted to evergreen [evergreen loans are those in which the principal amount and interest repayment keep getting postponed, sometimes through additional loans] in some ways to hide the bad loan, we were going to force them to come clean and that was the asset quality review process.'

'Did the scale of the problem shock you?' I ask.

'The size of the evergreening, it was significantly more than we expected,' he replies. 'This was partly because I had been reassured multiple times by the bankers, as well as by others, that I had privately tapped that this wasn't so bad. After our supervisors finished their clean-up jobs, the true scale was more alarming. Then I had to inform the finance ministry about it and I wanted assurances that we would have capital to deal with it. We created Rs 35,000 to 40,000 crores, which nobody remembers now, but the RBI effectively recapitalized the banking system from regulatory changes by about Rs 40,000 crores. We also needed government capital and the government was with us all along the way. So once we had done this careful analysis, the next step was to actually force the clean-up and then to start going after some of these habitual defaulters and get them to bring in more money, to sell some assets. What that whole process did was give bankers a backbone. Of course, that backbone has been reinforced by the bankruptcy code, but even before the bankruptcy code, we were starting to change the balance between bankers and promoters and bankers were no longer at the receiving end of promoter shenanigans,' Dr Rajan says emphatically.

Interestingly, the NPA issue and the lack of credit in the system is now being blamed on the previous government and Dr Rajan as RBI Governor. Niti Aayog chief Dr Rajiv Kumar blamed the slowdown in growth on Raghuram Rajan.

'There's enough blame to spread and that's why, I say, when anyone points the finger, there are always three more fingers pointing back at them. Interestingly, there are elements of the government that want to take credit for the clean up—acting finance minister Piyush Goyal after presenting the budget—and others blaming it for the slowdown. Clearly the problem starts with the structure of the public banking system. But this applies to the private sector too. A few private-sector banks like ICICI and Axis have pretty large bad loans too, and this has to do with the system itself. How do we tolerate a system where someone who borrows money doesn't have to pay it back? Then, when you examine the system and see the kinds of structures we've put in place, you'll see that they have been constantly gamed. For example, once we put the debt recovery tribunals in place, they started getting clogged up because there were more and more frivolous complaints by entrepreneurs. I was on a bank board as CEA and I was astounded that there were settlement offers coming in by someone who owed Rs 50 crores, who had offered a personal guarantee. But he had said that it would take us many years to recover it so why didn't we just settle it for Rs 2 crores. This is the kind of affrontery that I'd witness. We had to change the system because, in the first place, we didn't have a system where debt was considered debt and that the bank actually had the right to recover debt. It was a system where you only repaid your debt if you wanted to, nothing compelled you to do it, especially if you were a large promoter. There were many mechanisms to recover debt from the small guys but none for the bigger players. There were some habitual defaulters, who'd defaulted every ten to fifteen years, but they were billionaires and floating around in yachts. So, before one goes looking for corruption—and there was certainly some of that—we need to fix the system.'

'What about the charges of political pressure to give loans to key people despite them being known defaulters?' I say.

'Once again, some of if it could be corruption, but then again there is also genuine need for more infrastructure. We need more power plants, so the government might say please find a way to finance this guy because he's a successful promoter who's built successful power plants before. Just as today, the pressure is to go slow on Micro, Small and Medium Enterprises [MSMEs] because they are an important constituency for the government. These are pressures the government will apply without there necessarily being a sense of corruption behind it. Of course, the government owns these banks so the first line of defence against bad loans is the governance of these banks and if that hasn't worked, the primary blame sits with the government, not with the regulator. The regulator comes afterwards, and it is not equipped to see whether a loan is commercially successful or not. We have very little ability to do that. But we do have the ability to point out when the loan goes bad. So, if the regulator displayed forbearance and that forbearance didn't turn out to work, the regulator needs to shoulder some blame. Of course, the current government will ask why I succumbed to that previous government's request for forbearance, but on the other hand, they will ask me to succumb to their forbearance. It's very easy to look for scapegoats and even though I started the clean-up of the system in a big way, people will blame me for starting it too late. I've said this before—I couldn't start cleaning-up on day one, because we simply didn't have the tools to push those clean-ups from the bank. So, it's a process, and I think it's politically convenient to look for scapegoats, but you have to be careful doing it, because you also face the danger yourself.'

'In the years you were in India you also witnessed the movement against corruption and crony capitalism, the widespread belief that the UPA lost because of corruption scandals associated with it. How endemic do you think corruption is, how does it impact our economy and are we at a turning point in our tolerance for it?'

'The public tolerance is relatively low, but the questions are: Is it willing to act? Is there a widespread desire to act even on the personal account? This is important. How many of those who complain of corruption pay all their taxes? How many people are perfectly happy to point out a corrupt politician but won't take a bill because they want to evade service tax? That's petty corruption just like bribing a ticket conductor if you don't have the ticket. If we do all of the above and yet rail against grand corruption, we must realize that we're part of the problem.

'We have to work on multiple fronts. Cleaning up the financing of elections is extremely important because every election is a sham. Every party claims it spends below the limit set by the Election Commission, but all available evidence suggests the contrary. Why don't we move towards a more transparent system so that we don't have to finance elections with these off-the-balance-sheet items? I'm not a great fan of these non-transparent bonds that have been proposed because I want to know who's funding which party. I would think it very shady if an industrial house doesn't want to reveal how much it is funding a party. I think it should come clean. So, there's a lot of scope for reform, but it will only happen when the government has much less sway over the benefits to industrial houses. So long as the government controls credit, tariff, and advertisements to the press, it holds enormous levers of power which makes the private sector kowtow to its tune. How many private-sector people do you find criticizing the budget of any government? It is always splendid, wonderful, the best ever, God's gift to India! The reality is that crony capitalism starts from an overly controlled economy and from a dearth of self-made entrepreneurs. Many self-made entrepreneurs, who have made it without assistance from the government, tend to be more willing to speak their mind, more amenable to financing a variety of causes, not just those that are pleasing to the government.'

Speaking his mind while he was RBI Governor is perhaps what led to some tension with the Modi government as well. Unlike many other RBI governors, Raghuram Rajan toured and spoke to students at different universities about themes like social tolerance and the Francis Fukuyama principles of liberal democracy.

'First, you have to build a constituency for the policies you are implementing. You need to explain why you are doing it and you have to build constituencies,' says Rajan. 'I had to build a constituency for the banking-sector clean-up. Remember, there are strong vested interests who opposed this, and they will talk through their mouthpieces. Their mouthpieces will not acknowledge that they are being used but they will say that this clean-up is affecting growth, don't do it now. In reality, what they are saying is that we are affecting their patron. One way to deal with that kind of vested interest is to talk to the public and tell them why we need to do it. One of the important things I did is that I showed how the system of credit is slowing simply because of this accumulation of bad loans. It was slowing down before our asset quality review, so to blame the slowdown on the review itself was nonsense. I knew the criticism from the tools of the vested interests was going to happen,' he says, laughing wryly.

'The press are also looking for anyone who will speak. The bureaucrats don't speak. The opposition is always going to criticize. And the politicians in the ruling party are never going to criticize. So, the press needs someone who's in between, and if you are someone who's willing to speak, they're immediately going to read a lot into what you're saying. So, every speech I gave was parsed for what I was saying that could possibly be construed as critical of the government. Now, there were things that the government could be criticized about, but it wasn't my role to do so. My role was to talk about what could be done to push India forward. So, when in fact you do speak, sometimes you become a poster child of the Opposition even though that wasn't the intention. The press was looking for headlines. For example, at the IMF, when I was asked about how India was doing so wonderfully, I talked about all the good things we were doing but also said that India was like a one-eyed man in the land of the blind. It meant that India was doing a little better than everyone else. But the press made it out that I was criticizing the country! If I thought so poorly of the country, I wouldn't have been here,' Raghuram Rajan points out.

'My convocation speech at IIT, Delhi, on the importance of social tolerance for economic development was carefully crafted to mean that from an economic perspective, we would be crazy in India to give up our political debate, our ability to argue, our tolerance for free speech or for a back and forth. That's what some of these authoritarian countries needed to change and we're already there. We have a vibrant, flourishing democracy that's necessary for the next stage of development—to become an ideas economy. It would be silly to give all of this up when we're at the frontier, when we're innovating. The speech was a vehicle to emphasize India's history of tolerance. The speech was aimed at inspiring students. As a public official, it's very important to talk up the good things, you have to give people a vision,' he explains emphatically.

'Yet, many people thought that my speech was a criticism of the government. But I hadn't even mentioned the word "government" in my speech. So, this backlash was generated from people with really thin skins who had an idea of their government which was contrary to the vision that I put out. A week after my speech, I spoke to a senior government minister who told me that this was exactly what he'd been saying in all his speeches. So, the government itself wanted to portray the image of an India I'd talked about but the supporters of the government who started trolling me didn't understand it.'

'You left the US to return to India when asked by a former prime minister almost as a form of national service. By the end of your term, you had many voices from within the BJP asking for your ouster. At one point, you were called "mentally not Indian", and the prime minister did not extend your tenure. Did you leave India with a sense of satisfaction or a feeling of a job not fully done?'

'To say I came to India for "national service" implies a certain amount of personal sacrifice,' says Raghuram Rajan, dismissing this notion. 'These opportunities aren't sacrifices; they are really about self-fulfilment. Criticism is a very selfish thing. The benefits from doing these kind of activities are plenty. I mean, making a difference, there is no better feeling than making a difference, so I didn't think that I was here on sufferance. It's part and parcel of the role. There will be people who will oppose, sometimes in a language and terms that are not warranted, but I know where that's coming from. My family was a little upset by those kinds of things. But, as I've said many times before, I couldn't come to an agreement with the government on my continuing, and my term was over, so I had to leave,' he reiterates strongly. 'I think there's no greater satisfaction than being in India as the Governor of the RBI.'

From his tenure not being renewed to the furore over an RBI deputy governor's speech, the controversy over the RBI's powers and the abrupt resignation of Urjit Patel, it's been a dramatic time at the regulator's office. Does Dr Rajan, now as a distant observer, watching the turbulence from afar, feel like he has made a lucky escape?

He laughs. 'Well, I dealt with the same government. There are two things,' he says. 'First, time has moved on. We are closer to the elections now, and things change on that basis. But second, it's important to re-emphasize that the relationship between the RBI and the government is based on an enormous use of backchannels. You keep talking, you accommodate where you can and that gives you the ability to say "no" when you must. It's the constant thrust of give and take. It's a political job as much as it's an economic one. And when you look at what needs to be done, people don't realize you don't have the complete freedom to do it. You have to negotiate your way to solutions and that also makes the job interesting. It would've been much easier to deal with a total dictator because their word is final. That is not the case here.'

Raghuram Rajan came to India at a time of economic crisis and instability. Today, India is poised to become a three trillion-dollar economy, the fifth largest in the world. Where would Dr Rajan place India amongst global economies today?

'Today, political movements across the industrial West are emphasizing protectionism and I think that's a problem for India because we've still not got to the "Make in India" point that the prime minister has been emphasizing. We're still not internationally competitive on many fronts and we need to figure out how to get there. Despite the emphasis on Make in India, our exports have been in the doldrums for a while. We have to see what went wrong. Even though the US has put sanctions on China and people are moving operations away from it, India is not the first country they're thinking about moving to. We need to figure out what it will take to do that because currently the jobs numbers are horrendous. Employees Provident Fund Organisation [EPFO] numbers have gone up, implying that more people have joined the formal work force. The CMIE numbers, however, suggest that there has been no job growth for the last two to three years. This is where we really need to think about a massive restructuring of the economy, to revive the reforms that were seen as so urgent in the past, which we have slowed down on. Why aren't we expanding construction when we have such a great demand for infrastructure? How do we get rural industries to take off so that some of the people who were underemployed in agriculture can move into these industries? We shouldn't ignore the frustration expressed in the farmers' agitations, in the agitation of the Patidars, the Jats. We shouldn't ignore these early warning signals.

'That being said, we are doing reasonably well for a country at our level of per capita GDP,' he continues, 'but I think every Asian country has been through this phase, and we must realize that we need to do more. It's good that we're growing at 7 per cent but if we're not creating enough jobs, it will not be enough for our people. So, the cup is both half-full and half-empty. Let's not be pessimistic, we have come a long way to hit 7 per cent growth for twenty-five years. But at the same time, we should not be complacent because it's not enough for the employment needs of our people. The frustration could turn into rage if we're not careful, so we need to do far more. What we need to do is pretty obvious, but we need a sense of urgency about it and a national movement towards it, which, I hope, will happen soon.'

There we have it, a virtual economic manifesto for India from a man recognized as one of the brightest in the world. In his farewell speech to his RBI colleagues in 2016, Dr Rajan wrote, 'I will, of course, always be available to serve my country when needed.'

Will that opportunity arise again? Is there any truth to reports that he may be considered as finance minister if a Congress government comes to power? A tantalizing question left unanswered for now.

[7]

Nandan Nilekani

The Architecture of Aadhaar

Over 99 per cent adult Indians today have an Aadhaar card—a unique identification number for 1.2 billion people, one-seventh of the world's population. This project, once unimaginable in scale and ambition, owes its unique architecture and success to Nandan Nilekani. One of India's most successful and respected business leaders, co-founder of one of India's largest IT companies Infosys, Nandan Nilekani took his first step into public engagement when he worked as chairman of the Bangalore Agenda Task Force (BATF), a group of concerned citizens who worked with the state government on urban governance issues. Later, in 2004, when the UPA government came into power, the task force went on to pitch urban reforms in India to then prime minister Manmohan Singh and others. While many of those ideas became part of the first major National Urban Renewal Mission, it was in 2009 that a call from Rahul Gandhi effectively changed the course of Nandan's life, helping him transition from the corporate world to the world of governance. It enabled him to set up an identity project for every Indian on an unprecedented scale.[*]

---

[*] Interview conducted on 27 July 2018, Bengaluru

Non-executive chairman of Infosys, start-up mentor, founder of the NGO EkStep which helps millions of children with learning, and head of an RBI committee on digital payments, sixty-three-year-old Nandan Nilekani is on home ground in the heart of start-up India in Koramangala, Bengaluru. As we meet in his glass-walled conference room, the pleasant weather of Bengaluru seems a world removed from the heat and fury generated by the Aadhaar controversy. Nandan been accused of creating a surveillance Frankenstein by anti-Aadhaar activists. The Supreme Court has, however, decisively ruled on this and today in just under a decade, Nandan has had the enormous satisfaction of seeing his 'Mission Accomplished'—one that began under one government and was completed under a government completely ideologically opposite to its predecessor. This is a journey which began with one phone call.

'In 2009, I received a call from Rahul Gandhi,' Nandan begins. 'He called me on the day of the results, when the Congress came back with more seats.'

This was an unexpected second-term victory for the UPA government, with the Congress winning 206 seats.

'He asked me if I'd be interested in being the human resource development [HRD] minister of India? "We want somebody from another planet." I spoke to my colleagues at Infosys, and they all responded, "*Theek hai yaar.*" So I told him that I was ready to do it. On the day of the swearing-in of the new Cabinet, I was in Bengaluru. Now I didn't know these "fundas", that in politics, you have to hang around in Delhi and wait for your name to be announced. At 11 a.m. I received a call asking if I was in Delhi.

I mean, I'm an IT fellow, so I said no, I was in Bengaluru. They asked if I could arrive by 5 p.m. for the swearing-in and I told them that I didn't have a private jet. I then scrambled to see if I could find a plane to get to Delhi. Funnily enough, S.M. Krishna, who had been selected for the post of the minister of external affairs, was heading to Delhi. He too was in Bangalore but since his house was much closer to the airport, he managed to make it. In the midst of me trying to arrange a plane,' Nandan continues, 'Rahul Gandhi called again and said, "Sorry, it's not on." Later I realized that Mrs Gandhi probably felt I was a corporate type who wouldn't understand the poor and their problems. Dr Manmohan Singh, I think, felt I was a technocrat, not a politician and the HRD ministry would be too political for me to handle. It was a prime job—they weren't going to give it to some upstart from Bengaluru.' Nandan laughs. 'So, it was Rahul's idea, but they turned it down. I went back to my usual work.'

Convention prevailed and Kapil Sibal was eventually given the HRD ministry. But this gives a fascinating insight into the discussion that went into forming the UPA Cabinet in its second term and the dynamics between the top three. Rahul Gandhi, still relatively inexperienced at the time, was trying to push his out-of-the-box choice. However, fate had other things in store for Nandan because soon after, Prime Minister Manmohan Singh offered him a job at the Planning Commission. Nandan didn't think it was worth leaving Infosys to come up with five-year plans and told the prime minister just that.

'I wanted to do something active, operational, something that makes a difference. And the prime minister replied, "Okay, why don't you think about it and come back with an idea?"

'I began digging around and that's when I realized that the government had an identity project in the works. The Cabinet had approved the project in January 2009, and they were looking for someone to do it. Many people from the bureaucracy also wanted to work on it because it was a post-retirement cushy position. The more I studied the project, the more I realized its immense potential and how it could truly make a difference. In my book, *Imagining India* (2008), I had written in detail about how an ID system would help Indians, so I already had some background on the possible positive impact of the unique ID project. I had a few conditions though—the position has to be the equivalent of a Cabinet minister which was senior to the original ranking of minister of state. In Bangalore, it's okay but in Delhi, there's hierarchy—which level, how much clout and a Cabinet ranking position would give the necessary authority needed to get the job done. I had six or seven conditions, and the prime minister agreed to everything.'

'It's interesting that Manmohan Singh had the appetite for such a bold decision in 2009. Were you surprised?' I ask.

'The boldest bit wasn't Aadhaar—it was the notion of an outsider in a Cabinet rank,' says Nandan. 'To his credit, he agreed to my request immediately. He just did it. The file for clearance of this project was set to come to the Cabinet for approval the following week, on 26 June 2009, and the funny thing was that the bureaucrat who had been managing the file may have wanted the job after he retired. The file was moving quickly in the system. He was retiring on 30 June. He didn't know that there was an upstart gunning for the same job—nobody told him I was in the race! In the Cabinet meeting, Manmohan Singh proposed my name. He must have already spoken to a few key people like Pranab Mukherjee because they immediately agreed. The bureaucrat was shell-shocked.'

Fresh from Bengaluru and the pinnacle of corporate success, Nandan Nilekani arrived in Delhi, an outsider in the corridors of power. From day one, he knew if he wanted to make a success of it, he had to 'Bangalore' the way the bureaucracy functioned in Delhi.

'In government, you are defined by the size of your team (the number of joint secretaries who report to you) and the size of your budget,' Nandan says. The UIDAI organization had been designed

like the Election Commission with one Joint Secretary in every state.
That's thirty plus six in Delhi: thirty-six joint secretaries in total.
Perhaps, the Election Commission and the home ministry have that
many joint secretaries. It was a major coup that he had pulled to get
this approved for 1400 employees. I didn't need such big numbers
so I cut it down to 300. They were shocked; it was the first time in
the history of government that someone was *reducing* their budget.
Second, I wanted to bring in outside technology and talent because
while there are smart people in government, this project was going to
be tech-heavy. So, even though the headquarters was based in Delhi,
the technology team for the UIDAI was based in Bengaluru, where
it remains even today.'

Importantly, Nandan also wanted the tech team insulated from
the political battles he had to fight in Delhi so that they got the job
done with no outside interference. Some of the best technical talent
in Bengaluru contributed to the project with no or low salary because
it was for a national cause. It was also crucial to recruit the right
people in government like Ram Sewak Sharma (current chairman of
the Telecom Regulatory Authority of India [TRAI] or more famously
known as the man who took on Facebook founder Mark Zuckerberg's
'Free Basics' plan on grounds that it was discriminatory).

'At that time, R.S. Sharma was in the Jharkhand government;
he had just come back with a computer science degree from the
University of California and put in something completely unrelated
to computers, as is the usual system,' says Nandan, wryly. 'I got his
name from an exceptional IAS officer from the Karnataka cadre
K.P. Krishnan, who has an encyclopaedic knowledge of every
bureaucrat, and their strength and weaknesses. I invited Ram Sewak
for a meeting in Delhi. He said, "*Chalo*, let's do it," since he was
a risk-taker. Then I recruited a fine officer from the Indian Audit
and Account Services, K. Ganga, who was a terrific chief financial
officer. I got a brilliant young lawyer from the IAS, M.S. Srikar, as
my personal secretary to help me navigate the Byzantine corridors

of Delhi. So, I got a few key people from the government. There we were, a bunch of government people, a bunch of private guys who had never seen each other and me. Normally, there's a lot of mutual suspicion between private-sector people and government people. I had to overcome all those hurdles and blend the group together, not that we ever got it right since there was always some underlying friction, but at least because the task was so large, I was able to bring them all together.'

Now, Nandan Nilekani had a team but then came the next big battle—the turf war with the home ministry led by one of the UPA's most powerful ministers. One of Nandan's conditions when he joined was that there would be a separate Cabinet committee on the UIDAI—the first time it's ever happened. 'I think in fairness to the Congress leadership, the technical stuff may have been a bit arcane, but they trusted me and let me do my job. It was because I had complete freedom and trust from Mrs Gandhi, Dr Manmohan Singh, Pranab Mukherjee and Rahul Gandhi that I could get it done,' Nandan adds.

'Historically, identity has always been a function of the home ministry in any country. Identity is closely linked to citizenship and citizenship is awarded by the home ministry. They are the people who are supposed to keep illegal migrants out. When the home ministry realized that there was an upstart body being anchored in the Planning Commission who would be given the task to do identifications for the whole country—they were understandably livid. It took three years, from 2006–09, for the government to approve the UIDAI project because of these internal battles.

'The home ministry wanted to handle the identification verification or do all the enrolments while Nandan was insistent on executing all tasks related to the project, including enrolment, independent of the home ministry, worried that if UIDAI operated as just a "back office", they'd have no control. Finally, a partial compromise was reached—both teams would do 600 million people each. The home ministry would handle verifications in all the border states, including Uttar Pradesh and Bihar, and the rest would be handled by UIDAI.

'The first enrolment approvals we received were for 100 million people and we called it a pilot project. Only in India do you do something for 100 million people and call it a "pilot".' He smiles. 'The decision was taken when Mr Chidambaram had gone to Chennai, so it was approved in the prime minister's meeting. When he came back from his trip, I think he was unhappy that the decision was taken without him. When I was approaching the 100 million target, the home ministry was still not ready with their part of the project. So, I went to then finance minister Pranab Mukherjee and asked him what I should do. He wrote me a letter saying, "100 million pilot raised to 200 million", and this was approved by the Cabinet committee. So, now a 100-million pilot project had been increased to 200 million people.' Nandan grins. 'After reaching 200 million, the UIDAI quota was raised to 600 million. And we hit our target of 600 million in January 2009. So, I went back and asked them to increase it to 900 million.'

'So, politics taught you the opposite of what you had learnt in the corporate world?'

'There is politics in the corporate world, but of a different order and magnitude,' he says. 'See, I had no law behind me. I had no authority. I just had persuasion. I went to every state, every ministry—the RBI, Telecom Regulatory Authority of India, the World Bank—just evangelizing this idea to them.'

On his persuasion tour, Nandan recalls paying a visit to Arun Jaitley and Sushma Swaraj, the main opposition leaders of the BJP, but his biggest challenge was the then Gujarat chief minister Narendra Modi, who, in a twist of fate, would one day become the biggest advocate of Aadhaar.

Nandan recalls, 'Even though everything was ready to go in Gujarat, the chief minister Mr Modi had not approved the rollout.

Then I received a message to go and meet him and so I went to Gujarat. I thought, "I have to make this project successful, I can meet anyone",' he says.

The scheduled half-hour meeting went on for one and a half hours, and then the chief minister took pictures with Nandan Nilekani, which he later circulated.

'I guess they wanted to show people that I had gone to meet him. So, I sat there with him and he told me his life history—his take on 2002, his beginnings as a chai-wallah . . . everything. As soon as I left, he approved the project.'

'Did you ever feel frustrated that you had got caught in the middle of a political game?' I ask.

'This *is* the game. Reforms in India don't happen in a linear fashion. It is a two-step-forward-one-step-backward process. There are periods of high activity and those of complete inaction, but that is true of everything. That's the nature of politics. When there's a window of high activity, you get as much done as possible. When it goes into inaction, then you bide your time. Something will happen: the minister or bureaucrat will change. If you're playing the long game, you can deal with these kinds of things.'

To keep the UIDAI scheme out of politics, Nandan and his team also chose a name that was non-political. 'I didn't want some XYZ Yojana, so we carefully did a lot of research and found "Aadhaar", which means foundation; your identity is the foundation.'

More importantly, the word 'Aadhaar' worked in almost all Indian languages. But in attempting to escape politicization, Nandan explains how even the letter became political.

'The scheme's slogan is "Aam Aadmi ka Adhikaar" (the Right of the Ordinary Citizen). At the time, this was often used as a Congress slogan before the Aam Aadmi Party appropriated the "Aam Aadmi" metaphor. Only two people noticed it—Sonia Gandhi and Narendra Modi. When I met Mr Modi, he said, *"Aapne Congress ka slogan kyon use kiya?* [Why have you used a Congress slogan?]." Then one day

Mrs Gandhi told me she was concerned I was using BJP colours on the Aadhaar letter which was being sent to people, to which I said it was using the national flag colours. I had to get samples to show her that they were indeed the national flag colours. Here was a card going to a billion people so obviously one would be concerned about the text, symbols and colours on it. Yet, to my astonishment, only Mrs Sonia Gandhi and Mr Modi in the entire system asked me about it!' he says.

'I had made a commitment to Dr Manmohan Singh that I'll hit a target of 600 million enrolments before I leave. It was always a five-year term for me—one actually has only four years; the last year is for election stuff. Politically, you must assume that that's all you have. Fortunately, we reached 600 million in March 2009, so my job was done, and I put in my resignation.'

And then came a turning point for Nandan Nilekani and Aadhaar. The 2014 election and his decision to fight a MP election from his home seat, Bangalore South. He lost the election to the late Ananth Kumar of the BJP. Nandan's election defeat was probably his first failure in something he'd set out to do, an experience he recounts wryly. Even here Aadhaar had a role to play.

'In the 2014 elections, I was reviled by the BJP as the "Aadhaar man"—even Mr Modi came and campaigned against me and Aadhaar. Whatever. That's politics.'

Besides the personal defeat, however, the national defeat for the UPA was more worrying for Nandan and his vision for Aadhaar.

'I was nervous because there was no champion for Aadhaar,' he recalls. 'The official BJP position was to scrap it. The home ministry, which I had kept at bay all these years, suddenly saw a vacuum so they started moving in. Finally, I met the prime minister to discuss Aadhaar and its benefits to the country. Then he asked me the usual questions, one of them being if Bangladeshis could get it? I explained to him that it's not a citizenship number, it's an ID number. I told him that the scheme would save them a lot in targeting government benefits to actual users and that corruption would decrease. At the time, fortunately, oil rates were still high. So, the government was looking at savings. In the end, he became Aadhaar's biggest champion.'

The prime minister's backing of Aadhaar and his almost evangelical takeover created its own set of problems. The Congress quickly jettisoned it. After a journey that began with a call from Rahul Gandhi, now Nandan was the one making the call.

'I sent them a message urging them to own the project because it was probably the biggest achievement of UPA-2. But they didn't,' he says, making it clear he feels this was a wasted opportunity by the Congress.

'Now the Congress's stance is that the Aadhaar scheme which was for the development of the nation is now being used for surveillance. This is incorrect. On the other hand, I was surprised by Mr Modi's support and encouragement,' he admits.

However, the biggest battle for Aadhaar still lay ahead. While the Modi government made Aadhaar mandatory for everything from welfare schemes to PAN cards, mobile phones and even school admissions, the battle of public opinion raged furiously. Anti-Aadhaar activists believed that the scheme violated the Constitution and the Right to Privacy, that it was creating a surveillance State and, most importantly, that it excluded the marginalized from government welfare schemes. So, they took the case to the Supreme Court. However, on 26 September 2018, the Supreme Court ruled decisively that 'Aadhaar is constitutionally valid' and 'gives dignity to marginalized sections', although it struck down the right of private entities like banks and mobile companies to use Aadhaar data.

'Let me define the anti-Aadhaar ecosystem,' Nandan says. 'Those who are anti-Modi are anti-Aadhaar. This is the group which is politically motivated. Then there are those who believe it violates privacy. They ask why citizens should give their information to the State. The third group claims this is a surveillance project in the guise of a developmental one. If the government wanted surveillance on its citizens, they would use your phone because your phone is with you twenty-four hours a day. The State can read your messages, listen to conversations and know your location. If surveillance was the concern, there are other ways to do it. Aadhaar is not a great tool for surveillance,' he says.

Finally, there's the activist group, who claim that Aadhaar will lead to exclusion. Nandan however refuses to accept this argument.

'They believe the state should do everything, but they are not in favour of technology solving their problems. Their basic concern was that Aadhaar would be used for cash transfers into people's bank accounts rather than subsidized food rations. It is an ideological problem.'

Ironically, from the very beginning Aadhaar's aim was that of inclusion—so that even the man with no address, the one who lives on the street, has an identity.

'Our goal was that everyone should have the number and it should be easy to enrol oneself, which is why UIDAI created the world's largest enrolment platform. It can enrol 1.5 million people a day. At its peak, it had approximately 35,000 enrolment stations across India. It took between ten to fifteen minutes to enrol a person and one could do it any time, anywhere. Typically, in a government system, enrolment platforms will be in your hometown or village, where you'd have to visit at a particular time and wait for hours. Under Aadhaar enrolment, a person from Jharkhand working in Gurgaon could easily enrol themselves at an enrolment platform in Gurgaon on a Saturday afternoon. It was made very simple. Inclusion was a big part of it. One of the reasons Mrs Gandhi was such a big supporter of Aadhaar was because she also understood the "inclusion" point of view. I explained the process to her and showed her pictures of long queues of women at enrolment centres in Jharkhand. I expressed the demand there was for it. How women wanted it. Inclusion was the original design principle,' he says.

However, as the original architect of Aadhaar, Nandan does acknowledge that due to the push to make it mandatory, Aadhaar found its biggest opponents.

'When this government made it mandatory for PAN, bank accounts, phones to be connected to Aadhaar, the middle class turned against it. Suddenly, they were receiving messages from the bank every day to link their Aadhaar. I believe that if left to independent choice, Aadhaar will become the country's most common identification system because there is no other ID for a billion people. It is online and far superior to any other identification. For example, if a person needs to use an ID for a bank account and they can choose whatever ID they want, 90 per cent of people will still use Aadhaar because they don't have the other IDs that are needed. It wasn't necessary to make Aadhaar mandatory. Although,' he points out, 'it's not that I would've been consulted. I was just providing a platform. That kind of decision is taken at a different level.'

With the Aadhaar legal and political battle now closed, and over one billion Indians with an identity, what does Nandan Nilekani envision for the ID's future? How will it change India?

'Aadhaar's biggest asset is that it is completely egalitarian,' he says. 'Whether you are a billionaire or his driver—you get only one Aadhaar. There is no VIP Aadhaar. We are still realizing the potential of this unique ID. Today, 900 million bank accounts have an Aadhaar number attached to them. Six hundred million unique Aadhaar numbers are connected to bank accounts, and India runs the world's largest cash-transfer programme—several billion transactions have been done by the government into people's accounts till date. Three hundred million Jan Dhan bank accounts were opened largely because of Aadhaar. This is massive. It is an entire ecosystem.

'It affects the private sector too,' he points out. 'The reason Reliance could build JIO so fast was because they were enrolling at 1 million a day because the Aadhaar eKYC takes only two minutes.

So they could have people waiting at Dadar station [Mumbai] selling SIM cards. And you're only witnessing the beginning of this innovation. Aadhaar also enables people access to their own data. While there's all this talk about privacy, the real future is what we call data empowerment—people being able to use their own data to get better loans, better healthcare, better education,' he concludes. 'Internationally, people still can't believe India did this at this scale in less than a decade.'

It's been a long journey from India's IT capital to Delhi's corridors of power to interactions with states and people across the country. Now we come full circle, back to the city where it all began—Bengaluru, where the heart of Aadhaar, its technology, rests.

Nandan Nilekani turned a nascent idea into a reality that has redefined identity for Indians. Could this ID be the conduit for a universal basic income or universal healthcare, balanced with the individual rights of every Indian to recognition and ownership of their unique data one day? Perhaps it's then that Nandan Nilekani's work will be judged through a non-partisan lens as a crucial contribution to nation-building.

[8]

Aruna Roy

On Information as Power

A Ramon Magsaysay Award winner, a former civil servant, seventy-two-year-old Aruna Roy left the bureaucracy within a few years, setting up the Mazdoor Kisan Shakti Sangathan (MKSS) in 1987, which worked with farmers and labourers first in rural Rajasthan and then across India. It is in Devdungri, Rajsamand, in Rajasthan that she and leaders of the MKSS first found evidence of labourers not being paid their dues by government contractors for work done with no way to access the information of where the money was going. And it was here that the Right to Information (RTI) struggle was born. As a prominent leader of the RTI movement and part of the Sonia Gandhi–led National Advisory Council (NAC), Aruna Roy worked actively with the government to ensure this landmark legislation became law in 2005. This right gives every Indian citizen access to information regarding their government. In essence, it has transferred the power of knowledge to the people. She continues her fight to ensure the law isn't diluted in its implementation.[*]

---

[*] Interview conducted on 29 January 2019, New Delhi

When Aruna Roy and I meet, the first thing that strikes me is her warmth combined with a deep passion for her cause. It's a warmth which has forged her connection with India's most marginalized.

'In your life of public service, first as a bureaucrat and then as an activist, what do you think are India's defining moments?' I ask her.

'The defining moments for India's complex democracy,' Aruna Roy replies, 'have been when power has been asserted and seized by ordinary people, particularly the marginalized. Between 2005 and 2012, when rights-based legislations, like the Right to Information Act, the Right to Employment and the Right to Education, were passed in what appeared to be a refined understanding of democracy, it seemed as if India had turned a corner. The changing discourse of democratic governance, of the legitimacy of asking questions to those who govern us through the passage of laws for transparency and accountability, spoke of a people moving away from the fear of authority and favouring the power of truth instead,' she recalls.

'For those who had been at the receiving end of "India Shining" pre-2004, this seemed like a new beginning, promising more participation in the economy, and in governance. The marginalized majorities displaced Page 3, the glitterati, and, for a brief period, received equal space in the media and the public imagination. Facing overt, and covert, opposition from powerful forces, legislations like the RTI and MGNREGA [Mahatma Gandhi National Rural Employment Guarantee Act] have stood the test of time, despite a hostile regime, and are now backed by endorsements and demands from people and policymakers from across the world, to be expanded and deepened,' she says passionately.

'Also, crucially, the adoption of our Constitution on 26 January 1950, the drafting of which was led by Dr Babasaheb Ambedkar, was significant then, but is more so now. The values that it espouses, and the rights that it provides, inform and guide our work even today, and must continue to do so. It is both a guarantee and an immediate legal refuge for all citizens denied equality and justice. It is now, however, being systematically targeted by traditionally powerful groups, whose power is legitimized by hierarchies and power structures the Constitution seeks to abolish,' she points out.

Aruna Roy's engagement with the 'marginalized majorities' and her belief in constitutional justice and governance took root in her childhood. 'When India won its freedom (I was born a year before), it was an epochal moment. Non-violence and Civil Disobedience, as defining features during the struggle, had delivered us this freedom.'

Yet the communal strife that occurred during Partition left a deep impact on the young girl.

'I was too young to fully comprehend what was happening around me, but the killings, the sense of grief deeply impacted me. There are some cameos in my head—of someone wearing a Rampur cap [a fur cap usually worn by Muslims from Rampur] accompanied by tremendous cries of someone being beaten and tortured. After that, till I was seven or eight, if I saw anyone wearing a Rampur cap anywhere, I would turn hysterical,' she says. 'My mother took me to Mumbai in 1948, but when I got off the train, I screamed and screamed. My family didn't know what had happened to me, because I was quite a sober child. When they looked around, they found someone wearing a Rampur cap. When they asked me why I was screaming, I just sobbed, "Save him".' They had to take me to the man and he pacified me, telling me that he was fine, he was safe, urging me not to cry. And that became a family saga.' She smiles. 'It's that kind of response to senseless violence and killing, to labelling, to discriminating against people which is deeply ingrained in me. It's not just my politics, it's ME.'

Young Aruna went on to do brilliantly in her studies, graduating from Delhi's Indraprastha College in English literature and then trying her hand at teaching before sitting for the IAS examinations.

'I had a mother who was completely clear that wasting one's mind was the worst thing a woman could do. She had a brilliant mind; she was excellent at math and physics. But for various reasons, she never had a career and she regretted it terribly. I grew up with her, and her angst.' Aruna laughs.

'When I started teaching, I was soon unhappy with it. I was teaching English literature to a group of students who showed no interest in it at all, they were only interested in getting married and wanted a degree because it would help them make a better match; I, on the other hand, was passionate about my subject. So it was a mismatch. My father then persuaded me to take the civil services exam. I had always thought it was a babu service, but he convinced me that as a civil servant I could both travel around India and work. Of course, it wasn't easy to turn down the civil service once I had passed the exam in 1968. But as I went for training in Mussoorie and as the days went by, I became convinced that the brightest people were not necessarily from the IAS nor were they the most committed.

'Now, I may not have been the brightest either, but I was definitely committed to working for the people. I promised myself some time in the civil services because to dismiss something as irrelevant without experiencing it was wrong. The build up to the Emergency, which exposed the fact that the civil service buckled under power, resolved doubts, if I had any, and made me put in my papers in 1974 and I quit,' she says, smiling.

'It was while I was in the government though that I first got an idea of how powerful information is and can be. My decision to leave government was propelled by the inability to impact corruption and the arbitrary use of power within the system. And the "system" discouraged the sharing of information. Power as information became my primary matter of concern. And soon I became a part of the collective journey to change how information was accessed by people.'

Life and marriage to Bunker Roy, a social worker, then took her to rural Rajasthan. It was through her work in the MKSS with the villagers of Bhim, Rajsamand District in Rajasthan that Aruna's realization of how differently government corruption and the lack of information impact the poor was sharpened, as against the common perception of the urban middle class.

'Corruption plagues our society across class and sectors. Whether it is in posh sitting rooms, airports, or in chai *dukans*, village *chaupals* or gatherings, or second-class railway compartments, corruption is a topic of conversation. However, the economically marginalized are vulnerable in many more ways. In the forty-odd years that I have spent in rural Rajasthan, I have repeatedly been forced to recognize the critical nature of corruption, and its impact on the survival and liberation of the poor. In fact, the collective RTI journey was launched by daily-wage workers on government construction sites demanding their due (minimum) wages. They were called liars by the system, which claimed documentary proof for the number of days they had worked. When the overseers were asked to disclose the documents by the labourers and us, they took shelter under the Official Secrets Act [the act is used to protect government information mainly related to national security]! For them information is power, and those who have it guard it jealously. I cannot ever put away the memory of a "mate" (the overseer of a work programme) running away with the muster roll (the labour list) under his arm, afraid to show it to me and my colleagues. He later claimed that a cow ate it up! He and his brethren knew and guarded information with a virtuosity and dexterity born out of a knowledge of its power to control,' she says with a laugh.

Yet, battle by battle, stage by stage, the momentum grew. More and more activists, research groups, journalists and jurists joined in this information 'revolution'. In 1996, the first draft, by the Press

Council of the RTI, drafted by Justice Sawant, chairperson of the Press Council, was released in the public domain. Aruna remembers how it was people from rural India who spoke to the press that day, cutting through the official jargon.

'Thirty-eight-year-old Sushila was accosted by journalists who asked her what she, a rural woman, was doing at a press conference. She was asked if she had been to school. She said proudly: "Of course, till class 4." The journalist was dismissive and said, "How can someone like you understand or use the Right to Information?" Her answer was brilliant. "When I send my son to the market place with Rs 10 and he comes back, I ask for accounts. This country spends billions of rupees in my name, should I not ask for accounts? *Hamara paisa, hamara hisab* [Our money, our accounts]," she had replied. In four words she summed up transparency and the right to demand accountability. It cut through all the jargon and went straight to the heart of the matter.'

Aruna remembers the songs and poetry around this movement.

'Mohanji, a marginal farmer, worker, and an illiterate Dalit poet and lyricist sang: "*Pehle vale chor, jungalon mein rehte the. Aaj kal ke chor bungalow mein rehte hain—raj choron ka*" [The cheats of old times lived in the jungle. The cheats of today live in bungalows]. Another stanza of the song goes like this: "*Pehle vale chor bandookon se maarte the. Aaj kal ke chor kalmon se maarte hain—raj choron ka*" [The dacoits in the past used to kill us with guns. The dacoits of today kill us with a pen].

'The slogan and the song went "viral" (without the cell phone!) carrying with it a message that papers and documents held the key to our liberation from poverty, oppression and exploitation. This again spoke to people in their idiom an excellent lesson in communicating complicated political thought simply, elegantly so that people understand and own the concept.'

However, the challenge became to transform RTI from a people's movement into a political movement and finally into legislation.

They needed the government in essence to enact a law against itself. Did she ever think this would happen?

'It was a conjunction of many things,' she agrees. 'Corruption is a rampant and volatile issue. Honesty is a virtue we all want to claim, and the RTI occupied that moral space. It cuts across class though there was much political opposition. I remember a BJP lawyer telling us it will never happen in our lifetime. There were also many prominent supporters of our struggle who told us that we should be ready to accept that we would never see it in our lifetime.

'However, the RTI movement gained a life of its own, and when state after state—first Tamil Nadu in 1997, then Goa in the same year—passed a Right to Information bill, we were exultant. Other states followed like Rajasthan, Maharashtra and Karnataka in 2000, then Delhi, Assam, Jammu and Kashmir. And once people started realizing the practical value of this law, there was no taking it back,' she says.

Pressure grew on the Central government as well with a writ filed in the Supreme Court to bring in a national RTI law. However, in 2002, the RTI Bill was passed in Parliament as the Freedom of Information Act—a weak and watered-down law. It wasn't even notified and had no penalty provisions or an independent appeals mechanism. It was then, as the movement approached all political leaders, that they found their most prominent supporters in Sonia Gandhi and the Left.

'The Central government enacted a lousy law, so we bargained for a better one. What convinced Sonia Gandhi is her immense sympathy for the disadvantaged. I realized this more with every meeting of the National Advisory Council. Her concern for the poor is genuine, and it strongly affects her decisions. She realized that transparency would benefit those at the bottom of the pyramid. She asked all the Congress states to implement it,' Aruna recounts. 'The promise for a national RTI law was then included in the UPA manifesto and in the National Common Minimum Programme too.'

In 2005, the movement finally achieved hard-won victory. The new Right to Information Act was passed unanimously in Parliament. The NAC headed by Sonia Gandhi with members like Aruna Roy, M.S. Swaminathan, Jean Drèze, Jairam Ramesh and others was set up with the aim to advise the Manmohan Singh government on social policy.

Aruna Roy recounts, 'The National Advisory Council headed by the UPA president Sonia Gandhi with a range of non-government domain experts was created to implement the National Common Minimum Programme (NCMP). This was a trajectory of "good" governance—first a manifesto, then a statement of commitment, then a body to monitor its implementation by the government. The NAC offered a platform for demanding and putting in place a system of transparency and accountability.'

However, it soon became a focus of much controversy with the Opposition attack on the Sonia Gandhi–led NAC as a parallel power centre to Prime Minister Manmohan Singh and his Cabinet or 'Super Cabinet'. These are charges Aruna Roy vociferously denies.

'It was not a parallel power centre. It only had a right to look at social policy, nothing else. Even on the matter of social policy, the NAC simply drafted a legislation or policy and sent it to the government. It was the government that passed the law. The problem is that the NAC was never clearly explained and structured, so it always lived in a state of limbo, with lack of clarity of its structural tethering,' she points out.

Feeling that she had lost touch with reality in 2013, Aruna once again left for Rajasthan to continue her work there and understand shifting values in the growing numbers of youth under twenty-five.

And though it is the UPA government she engaged with so closely, working within the NAC and bringing in the RTI law, today, ironically, she is opposed to another UPA-era legacy, the Aadhaar act. To this, she goes on to say, 'It is not ironical. An activist speaks for the Constitution and the people, not for a party. I was never an employee of the government nor a party member. All of us retained our right to freedom of expression and I, along with others, wrote public letters to the PM and criticized government policy. In fact, before I joined the NAC, I met Mrs Gandhi and told her it would be difficult if I did not have the right to dissent with the UPA on issues. She said I could, and steadfastly allowed me the freedom to speak critically of the UPA; a stark difference with the current dispensation's restriction on freedom of speech. I opposed the Aadhaar in all public discussions and in special meetings. I was not a member of the government nor the party and had the freedom to dissent and disagree.'

'I find this an interesting contradiction,' I say, 'because when I interviewed Nandan Nilekani for this book, his vision for Aadhaar, like yours for RTI, is that of empowerment for the marginalized, in the case of Aadhaar by giving them a unique identity.'

'Not at all,' she disagrees vehemently, 'there's a conceptual and practical conflict between RTI and Aadhaar. RTI asks the State to be transparent to its citizens, whereas Aadhaar asks the individual to be transparent to the State. Why should the State know everything about me? I, on the other hand, need to know everything about the State because I, as sovereign, created the State. I have created the State as a citizen. If you examine the facts in Rajasthan, this mystique of the number, this mystique of technology has, in reality, brought an extreme denial of the right to live. Three lakh names were struck off the rations list in Rajasthan. If a handicapped or an elderly person could not reach a point of verification, many were declared dead! Once you are declared dead, you lose all identity and access to all social-security benefits such as rations, etc.

'Also, by making digital identities like Aadhaar mandatory, the government has gathered incredible amounts of detailed data on every citizen. The government claims the right to protect this data and uses this smoke screen to become the exclusive custodian of data and information. This is a new avatar of the Official Secrets Act, but with greater controls and more questionable methods of operation, which is exactly what the RTI was set up to fight,' she concludes.

Has the RTI today become embroiled in politics? I ask. Many of the RTI applications often seem to be about political battles. For example, a RTI petition asking about the prime minister's educational degree or trivial queries such as the number of cups of tea served at a government office.

'Whatever the reason, even if its political,' she says emphatically, 'I have the right to know whether my prime minister is fibbing or not. I have a right to know where he got his degree from. I have a right to know what the degree says. For example, if I state that I am from Indraprastha College and I have a master's degree in English, everyone in the world has a right to know if my statement is true. However, they don't have the right to know whether I had a quarrel with my husband; that's in the private domain.

'Especially within our representational democracy,' she continues, 'information is key. The Association for Democratic Reforms has established that all those standing for elections reveal their assets and criminal history, if any. However, the new "secret" electoral bonds[†] are a setback. They make election funding opaque and reduce disclosure about crucial questions such as the influence of money on elections. Now, it will not be possible to track foreign and Indian corporate donations to political parties and understand which corporates are influencing a party's agenda. This harms the basis of representational democracy, and sovereignty itself,' Aruna Roy points out.

Today, the RTI movement has come a long way. An estimated eighty lakh applications are received in a year. But the journey ahead

---

[†] Announced by the NDA government in 2017, individuals or corporates can buy electoral bonds from banks to donate to political parties. The bonds will not bear the name of the donor essentially making their identity anonymous.

rests on the role of the ordinary Indian, the *aam aadmi* (*insaan* or *aadmi* and *aurat*), who made it possible in the first place.

'It is ordinary folk who carried the movement on their shoulders,' she says. 'They offered us everything they had; they opened up their homes to us, generously shared their food, and came and sat at dharnas at the cost of losing their wages on those days they were agitating for the cause. The *safai karamchari* [sweeper] who cleaned the road where we sat for our dharna in Beawar in Rajasthan donated Rs 10 from his daily earnings to our dharna. An eight-year-old boy working for two hours in a medical shop opposite the site gave Rs 2 out of the Rs 8 he earned every day. Almost ten years later, when the law came into force, we gathered at the same spot to mark the occasion. The boy, now a young man, sought us out and said, "Do you recognize the young boy who used to give you Rs 2 every day? I want to file one of the first RTIs today. I feel as though this is my law!"' She smiles at the memory.

'However, there are currently subversive efforts underway to dilute the law.[‡] Information commissions which have been set up to look at complaints are kept understaffed, leading to rising backlog of appeals.[§] Even though the RTI act says the information commissioner's stature, authority and compensation must be at par with those of an election commissioner's, the current government says they will decide this,' Aruna Roy points out.

'And even when the RTI applications are answered, there are new challenges. Over seventy RTI petitioners have been killed and many more have reported harassment or assault. The challenges intensify with the struggle. Every Indian who is stopped from the right to expression must recall Subramania Bharati's poem. The

---

[‡]   https://thewire.in/rights/rti-law-dilution-information-commission
[§]   https://economictimes.indiatimes.com/news/economy/policy/govt-seeks-control-of-info-commissioners-salaries-term-through-rti-act-amendments/articleshow/65027774.cms

poem is about an old woman who is dying of hunger. She needs gruel to survive; but more importantly she needs the right to say she needs gruel,' Aruna says.

'Do you think a campaign like the RTI could have worked today,' I ask, 'when the words "activists" and "activism" are often used in a derisory manner?'

'Anyone who acts on an idea for public good is an activist. A musician, a writer, a TV producer, and even the prime minister could turn into an activist tomorrow,' she replies. 'Activism also assumes a certain moral and legal integrity. And that is the space, I think, which is contested because others want to occupy that space. Today, even though people are behind bars, being called Urban Naxals (for example, the lawyer and activist Sudha Bhardwaj and the poet Varavara Rao), and others are being threatened, the bottom line is that people don't doubt their integrity. Most people don't even know who Naxals are—they just think it's a bad word.

'As for me, it's my strength and confidence in my beliefs that is important. I have it for various reasons. I am a privileged Indian in every way. I have the right education, and access to power. If I don't have the courage to stand on my feet and fight against oppression, I will be guilty. At a personal level it will be the end of my life. If I withdraw from activism, I will be betraying my innermost belief in ethics. So long as activism has a constitutionally sound normative base, it does not matter what people have to say about activists. That's why the Constitution of India is so important and the Preamble is like a prayer to me,' she concludes.

Aruna Roy and the movement she drove achieved the impossible in a decade. The RTI Act is a transformational law for the people of India. However, it is the many challenges that lie ahead, the dangers to constitutional values, and a truly participative democracy, she says, that still drive her crusade every day.

[9]

Aamir Khan

Star Power and Social Change

Aamir Khan is a superstar who is changing India in his own way and on his own terms. It's this conviction that has led him—one of the famed Khans who has ruled Bollywood for almost three decades with hits like Qayamat Se Qayamat Tak, Lagaan, Rang De Basanti, 3 Idiots, Dangal, *among others—to break free from the shackles of stardom and use it for social change. Switching with unprecedented ease between his work as a Bollywood actor and activist, Aamir Khan refuses to be hemmed in by definitions of what a star can or cannot do. He sees no contradiction in starring in movies with Amitabh Bachchan and Katrina Kaif, in his last release* Thugs of Hindostan, *side by side with performing shramdaan (contribution through labour) in Maharashtra's remote villages with his Paani Foundation.*[*]

---

[*] Interview conducted on 4 August 2018, New Delhi

The first thing I notice about Aamir Khan is that he wears his superstardom lightly—no entourage, no airs, no make-up person fussing around him. As he greets me in his hotel suite in Delhi, his handshake is firm, and he is the sort of person who looks you in the eye. As we sit across from each other, the indelible impression I have is—here is a man comfortable both in his skin and conviction. At fifty-four years, he is also a believer—in his craft, his talent, his choices and, most importantly, his causes.

Aamir's belief in himself didn't come easily. After the runaway success of his debut film, *Qayamat se Qayamat Tak,* in 1988, the young actor, just twenty-three at the time, was offered a host of movies to sign, but the directors he dreamt of working with still hadn't reached out to him. While popular stars were acting in forty films at a time, Aamir thought he was being selective by signing on only ten movies. Once he began working on the movies though, he realized the reality was very different from what he had signed up for.

He recalls, 'That one year was very traumatic for me. It was like torture on the sets because I knew I was doing bad work. I chose my films based on the scripts but when I started shooting, I realized the vison I had and the one the director and the producer had were completely different. So, if the script said mountains, I would envisage Kashmir, the director would be talking of Khandala and the producer would say Film City!'

Then, one after another, the films began to release and Aamir was not surprised when they flopped.

'I had four flops in a row and was being dismissed as a "one-film wonder". I used to go home and cry because I was so miserable,' he says. 'I felt like I was sinking in quicksand and nothing could save me. Then, out of the blue, I got a call from a director I truly respected and wanted to work with—Bhatt Saheb, who was one of the biggest names in the film industry at the time. I met him, convinced this was my lifeline, and finally I would be part of the cinema I wanted to do. And then, disaster . . . I hated the script.

'That night,' Aamir remembers, leaning forward to stress his point, 'was a turning point in my life. My big dilemma was if I compromised with my beliefs now, the rest of my life would be a series of compromises. Yet, once I took my decision, it gave me strength. I knew that if I didn't compromise now at my worst, at a time when I was facing professional death, I wouldn't have to ever compromise my beliefs again. So, the next morning, I told Mr Bhatt: "Sir, I would love to work with you, but I can't do this movie. I don't like the script."'

Fortunately, Mahesh Bhatt took the rejection sportingly and they eventually worked together. More importantly, as Aamir says, 'It set the path for all my choices after that—my conviction that I won't let go of what I believe, no matter who asks me.'

Aamir's unshakable belief in himself and his choices, as opposed to adhering to the latest Bollywood trends, has produced some of the best films in Indian cinema. His film *Lagaan* in 2001—a celluloid saga about a small Indian village taking on a British regiment in a game of cricket . . . and winning—became the second Indian movie to be nominated at the Oscars. This uplifting tale of victory against all odds went on to become one of the biggest grossers of its time.

Yet, what stands out for Aamir about the film—as a first-time producer—is the single schedule of six months it was shot in and the use of sync sound, both unheard of in mainstream Bollywood at the time. All top actors were used to rushing from set to set, often in the same studio complex, because they were shooting for different movies simultaneously. In contrast, Aamir and his team headed to a village in Bhuj in Gujarat, staying there for the full six months of shooting. His decision to shoot the entire film in sync sound was also extremely unusual.

'I just couldn't deal with shooting a dramatic scene on the sets and then reproducing the same emotion in a dubbing studio with no co-star to react to, in a completely different mind space. However, sync sound was a complete no-no for mainstream Bollywood at the time. I remember at a party, Adi Chopra and Karan Johar told me I was crazy to try this in the first movie I was producing.'

Being told he's 'crazy' has never been a deterrent for Aamir though and, he grins as he points out, he set a trend in Bollywood.

'Every mainstream movie is shot in sync sound today . . . and all in one schedule,' he says.

Aamir's career graph continued to soar. He starred in hit after hit like *Rang De Basanti* (2006), *Ghajini* (2008), *3 Idiots* (2009). His 2016 film, *Dangal*, a story about an overweight retired wrestler living his unfulfilled dreams through his daughters, broke box-office records in India and went on to become the highest-grossing Indian film internationally as well. Its success was especially phenomenal in China.

Aamir laughs as he describes his China following, 'It actually began with *3 Idiots*. Hindi movies didn't usually release in theatres there, but it became popular in China through websites which show pirated prints of movies, mainly because of the story—the burden of educational pressure on students—which struck a huge chord there. It went viral because Chinese kids were watching and showing it to their parents, all on these websites. Then, *PK* became a super hit as well again on these pirated websites and by the time *Dangal* was released, I had become so popular, it got a theatre release in China, where it was a smash hit. What's fascinating,' he continues, 'is that I got the same reaction from Chinese viewers as I did from Indian viewers. It's about the common language of cinema and human emotions.'

Luckily for Aamir and Indian cinema, most of his choices have been not just critically acclaimed but also huge commercial hits (*Thugs of Hindostan* being an exception). But he is adamant that he bears the cost of his decisions—good or bad.

'My choice to do a film is completely creative,' he says, 'I loved the scripts of *Taare Zameen Par, Dangal*, so I chose to do them. Once that choice is made, though, I try to make sure my decisions are economically viable. I ensure no one loses money because of my choices. I don't take a rupee for any of the films I work in; if the film makes profits and everyone recovers their money, I get a share. If not, I take the hit.'

Given that the fee of a superstar like Aamir Khan would be an estimated two hundred and fifty crore per film, the fact that he does this means he literally puts his money where his mouth is—luckily, it's a formula that has been hugely successful for him so far. An exception was the recent *Thugs of Hindostan*, produced by Yash Raj Films, which was a box office disaster. How does he respond to failure? I ask.

'I went wrong with *Thugs of Hindostan*,' he replies. 'Every failure has taught me a lot. I've learnt a lot from Thugs too.'

For an actor so immersed in his art and films, why then would he choose to transition into a completely different world of social causes? Why did he feel the need to do so?

'I think it's actually something I imbibed from my mother,' he says, taking a long, ruminative drag of his cigarette [he has given up smoking since this interview]. 'I was very good at tennis when I was growing up. I played at the Maharashtra state level and regularly won tournaments. Every time I came home from a tournament, my mother would ask me how it went, and I'd proudly answer that I had won and show her the trophy, she gives me a hug and I'd go to sleep happy. One day, I came back with yet another trophy and after she hugged me, she said softly, "I wonder what the mother of the boy who lost is feeling right now. He must have come home dejected and low. She must be consoling him right now, as we speak."

'My mother wasn't trying to make me feel bad about my victory,' Aamir points out animatedly, 'she was genuinely thinking about that mother and her son. But her words stayed with me. In life, our wins are often at the cost of some unknown person's defeat. The other person is not a mere competitor; he is as much a flesh-and-blood human being as me—he has his own family, his own aspirations and dreams. Of course,' Aamir laughs, 'I still didn't give up my winning attitude on the tennis court, but I had greater empathy for those I was playing against.

'The other person who really influenced me was Satyajit Bhatkal,' Aamir continues. 'We were both friends at Bombay Scottish, we asked the same existential questions,' he says, chuckling. 'So were drawn to each other. Satya was a very good student, he always came first in class, while I was an average student. We all thought he'd make it big. But Satya didn't join the corporate world. Instead, he chose the social sector. He would distribute pamphlets at railway stations, for various causes. His paper had a circulation of few thousands, but he just kept doing it even though no one would pay him much attention. Every time we met, I'd ask him what he was doing, and he'd tell me of his social work and I'd tell him about my career in the movies. It made me think—I have so much and what am I doing to help people? It used to bother me, and as I became more successful, it began to bother me even more.'

And then out of the blue, Aamir was offered the chance to host a game show produced by Star Plus. Now, this was the time when reality TV meant shows like *Big Boss* but for Aamir, the offer got him thinking about an entirely different reality: how he could engage with issues he cared about and to use the 'Aamir Khan' brand, in a sense, to bring systemic problems pertaining to India, its politics, social stigmas, gender roles, caste violence, etc., centre stage in Indian homes.

'I called Satya and told him: "You've been working for so many causes for the last twenty-five years, nobody listens to you. *Shayad meri sun le* [Perhaps, they will listen to me]. But I will only do this, a show like *Satyamev Jayate,* if you come on board with me." It was a

2 Defining India

chance to use the power of my voice for a greater good.' (Satya went on to head the research team for *Satyamev Jayate* and is currently the CEO of Aamir's Paani Foundation.)

Of course, being Aamir Khan meant he had a set of non-negotiable conditions. 'I called Uday Shankar who was heading Star [*sic*] and said I won't do the game show, but I have another show in mind, *Satyamev Jayate*.'

'However, I wanted to talk to India through this show and India is a country of multiple languages. So, my first condition was that the show must air across the bouquet of Star channels in regional languages and if, in a certain region, the Star channel was not number one, the show must air on the number one channel,' Aamir says with a laugh. This meant that in Andhra Pradesh, *Satyamev Jayate* actually aired on Star's competing channel and not Star. And in Hindi besides Star Plus, Aamir insisted the show be shared with Doordarshan for its reach in the villages of India.

This meant that for the first time, a television show was being broadcast in Hindi and several regional languages across different competing channels at the same time. It is absolutely unprecedented for TV channels to share content, however the bemused channel head wanted Aamir Khan, so he agreed. But there was one thing he strongly advised against.

'He told me that 11 a.m. on a Sunday is considered graveyard time on TV. No one watches TV at that time. He asked me to change the slot to prime time. But I was clear I didn't want people watching serials for ten minutes, news for five minutes, and Aamir Khan for ten minutes. I remembered Sunday mornings was when India used to come together to watch *Ramayan* on TV,' he said. 'And I wanted that. Either watch me properly or don't watch me at all.'

Satyamev Jayate scripted TV history. Its ratings went through the roof and for the first time in Indian television, never-before-discussed subjects found screen time on a general entertainment channel.

The show's very first episode focused on female foeticide and it involved mothers talking about how they were forced to abort their female foetuses. The impact was immediate and real. Both the Rajasthan and the Maharashtra governments ordered crackdowns on illegal ultrasound clinics after the show was aired. The chief justice of the Rajasthan High Court ordered a fast-track court for hearing illegal cases of foeticide. A central child helpline received 40 lakh calls after the episode on child sexual abuse was aired and an estimated four lakh people became members with Alcoholics Anonymous (AA) in just a month after the show on alcoholism—this when the average membership before that was just 35,000.

'In fact, today,' Aamir says, 'the NGO we worked with on the show just informed us that Rajasthan has achieved its target of becoming gender neutral—the same number of baby boys and girls are being born in the state. That's change you can see on the ground. I don't make any false assumptions that I can change the country or society . . . But, yes, I can tell a story, make people aware, I can touch people's hearts, make them see what they had turned away from. No single individual can be the harbinger of instrumental change. It is always a collective process, but always remember, when you give people information, you give them a peculiar power that can go a long way in making things change for the better.'

As we talk, Aamir is almost evangelical about the impact of *Satyamev Jayate*. On air, it was clear the show affected Aamir personally, very deeply. He often broke down during episodes while listening to people tell their stories. The experience changed him.

'I cry very easily,' he says. 'Crying, like laughter, is a way to express your feelings, so I don't curb my emotions. When I feel like laughing, I laugh. When I feel like crying, I cry. *Satyamev Jayate* made me realize, on a much deeper level, what is happening in our society and in our country. I've met people from across the country, from villages to cities, people who are champions of causes. In every case, not only me but my core team, which included seven people, would go through the research material. There were always so many hard facts coming out, it would be very hard for us to absorb and digest them.

'After my first season, I actually went into depression for a very long time. I couldn't function properly,' he says sombrely. 'When I was in conversation with friends, I would suddenly break down, and it took me a good year or two to get out of it. Kiran, my wife, would just hold me then.' He smiles. 'It helped that when I was going through the material, Azad would be sitting on my lap, so slowly I came back to normalcy.'

But, more importantly, the team found hope in tragedy.

'We came across people with no financial strength or political power, or any other power, but their *inner* strength and courage was so huge, they were able to face up to the most difficult situations and still be happy. And people like this would inspire us and bring back hope.

'Let me give you an example,' he recounts. 'We did an episode on honour killings and there was a story about Babli and Manoj, two people from the same *gotra* in the Jat community, who were brutally killed by Babli's family members who opposed their marriage. Manoj's mother and sister came on my show. They were from a small village in Haryana, people there had completely stopped talking to them, communicating with them, nobody sold them anything, they couldn't even buy the *kalash* [urn] for Manoj's ashes from the village. When they made a police complaint, they were threatened, then asked to name the price they wanted to withdraw the case, politicians even came to their house to "settle" the matter. Yet, they did not succumb to any pressure. Staying in their house, alone, in that same village, they took the case to the very end till the murderers were convicted.

'In contrast, look at us in Mumbai. If a bandh is declared by any political party, we sit at home with the doors closed and windows shut; we're all terrorized by it. And we are educated, privileged people. We assume women are weak, rural women are powerless, but I don't know where people like Manoj's mother get the strength from; she is illiterate, but she broke every stereotype. These are the people that gave me hope.'

In many ways, *Satyamev Jayate*, which put the spotlight on issues like female foeticide, rape, domestic violence, criminals in politics, marked an apogee in Aamir's journey towards becoming the social star-activist he is today. A show hosted by a superstar on real-life social and political issues was groundbreaking.

The impact and change, from identifying and researching problems and witnessing the response from government and social agencies, caused by *Satyamev Jayate*, led Aamir to transition to another first for an actor. Taking a cue from Mahatma Gandhi's famous lines, he wanted to be the change he wanted to see, and set up the Paani Foundation, a people's movement to reduce the impact of drought in Maharashtra. Through this, Aamir and his team aim to empower villages with knowledge and training in watershed management to eradicate drought, and they also use the Gandhian concept of shramdaan, involving the entire community. The foundation then organizes competitions between the different villages for prizes in water management with a Satyamev Jayate Award for the best village (perhaps some life lessons from *Lagaan* here).

'All people need water,' says Aamir, as he outlines his vision of what the Paani Foundation has set out to achieve. 'This common goal turns out to be a great unifier. In fact, in one village, there was a very closely contested, bitterly fought election every year for a local body. One time, it was clashing with our competition for the best village in water management. The same people who were meant to be working together as a team for this were going to be contesting each other in this local election, leaving them with little time to prepare for anything else. Finally, one of the villagers suggested a solution: let's have *one* common candidate whom we all vote for; no fighting, no party affiliations, and let's agree on a consensus right there and then. And that's what happened—water came first, not politics,' he says with a smile.

Today, the Paani Foundation, which began with 116 villages in three talukas of Maharashtra, is working with 4025 villages across seventy-five talukas, in just three years. A crucial intervention at a time when the state is reeling from successive years of drought.

'Why has shramdaan, the Gandhian philosophy of service to society through labour, particularly inspired you?' I ask.

'Shramdaan,' Aamir replies, is 'one of the foundation's pillars, and the reason we include it is as part of our project is to get people together. There are differences and divisions in our country based on so many things like caste, politics, religion. We felt that when people come together and work physically for a common cause, it unifies you. It doesn't matter what caste, community or religion you belong to, when you work together in the hot sun towards a common goal.'

One of the people who have joined in the shramdaan and has been the foundation's biggest supporter has been Maharashtra chief minister Devendra Fadnavis whose administration, Aamir says, from collectors to local *tehsildars*, have backed the initiative wholeheartedly. Interestingly though on the day of the Satyamev Jayate Cup, where villagers came from across the state for the award, Aamir Khan invited the chief minister and leaders of all political parties from the Sena, Nationalist Congress Party (NCP), and Congress on stage together. 'They wanted to send a larger message—for water, all the political parties of Maharashtra are one. So, whether it's the chief minister, the foundation's funders like Reliance Foundation, Tata Trust, the HT Parekh Foundation, Rajiv Bajaj, they have been my biggest supporters and stood by me and my vision for the Paani Foundation. Every one of them has made an integral contribution,' Aamir tells me.

How does Aamir himself balance his different worlds and their contradictions? From Film City to rural India, from a world of dry wells to the world of Jacuzzis, does the reality of Mumbai and the film industry seem illusory compared to the reality he's now seen?

Aamir pauses as he frames his answer. 'I understand that there is no *one* reality in the world; there are so many realities and you don't regard them as one. The fact is that life has contradictions; that is the reality of life. I don't think any world is less real than the other,' he replies. 'The world of cinema is a make-believe one, but the story we're telling in the film is real and how it affects people is real. *Taare Zameen Par* had a huge impact on people. Cinema has a huge ability to affect minds and hearts. Typically, I do movies which are close to my heart, so for me both worlds are real.'

As we talk, Aamir Khan in person—just like in his movies and activism—is a complex mix of different characteristics. He is self-confident without being arrogant, he has a passionate earnestness and youthful sincerity which belies his years, and strength of conviction without worrying about real-world factors like consequences. While Bollywood insulates actors from, say, religious identity—whether your last name is Khan or Kapoor, what matters is how you fare every Friday—in today's India, even Aamir Khan is accused of 'love jihad' or reminded that he is a Muslim if he raises concerns about ongoing incidents of mob violence.

'What about the downside, Aamir, of getting into areas that can be controversial?' I ask. 'Your film *Fanaa* suffered when you spoke about the rehabilitation of those displaced by the Sardar Sarovar dam; when you spoke about intolerance, you were told to go to Pakistan and lost your endorsement for Snapdeal.'

'I respond to the trolls with love. I try and understand where they're coming from. I refuse to let it affect me or my beliefs. My job is to communicate,' he adds. 'But I've learnt to choose my words carefully . . . on what to say where and when.'

'It's sad that you should have to censor yourself, in that case,' I interrupt.

He laughs wryly. 'Come on, except for a few journalists, is anyone speaking out today? Let's get real.'

An unpleasant reality that more and more public figures are facing today. However, Aamir isn't letting the background noise change his core convictions. So, from superstardom to public service—could politics be the next transition? He's already been asked by the government's main planning body, the Niti Aayog, to make a presentation on how his Paani Foundation could work in other states and has deposed before a parliamentary standing committee on the problem of overpriced foreign drugs, after a *Satyamev Jayate* episode focusing on this.

'Are these the first steps to a political role?' I ask.

He shakes his head immediately. 'Never. For me, the greatest contribution to nation-building is being a creative person. Throughout history, it's the poets, the artistes, who have shaped the cultural and social fabric of a nation. That's what I am and will continue being. I don't think being a politician can replace that. I am using my craft to communicate that we can solve the most pressing problems of our times,' he replies.

So, for now Aamir Khan will continue to balance his many identities—superstar, activist, husband, father and son—effortlessly for those who are watching. But how does he view himself?

'I'm a human being who's struggling to make sense of what is happening around me,' he says.

Even though it's nice to hear he has something in common with the rest of us, the reality is that Aamir Khan has made an extraordinary life transition, doing what no star has ever done before—a unique partnership of star power and activism on the ground. In defining himself, Aamir has redefined Indian cinema and social change.

[10]

Kamal Haasan

The Unmaking of an Actor, the Making of a Politician

*The unmaking of an actor, the making of a politician, the Dravidian movement and 'Empress Jayalalithaa' are all key defining factors for Kamal Haasan—the sixty-four-year-old actor par excellence now aims to be Tamil Nadu's next chief minister. An avid reader, a student of world cinema and philosophy, he seems far removed from the Machiavellian world of intrigue, back-room deals and rampant corruption that has come to be associated with realpolitik. Yet Kamal Haasan insists that he is not a naive debutant, but a man whose time is set to come on the Tamil Nadu and national political stage.**

* Interview conducted on 9 December 2019 when Haasan was in Chennai

As we begin our conversation, he traces his journey back to where it began. Kamal Haasan was born in a Brahmin family from Chennai, almost as an 'afterthought', as he puts it.

'I was a late child in the family. My eldest brother, Charuhasan, was twenty-four years older than me. After him came the late Chandra Hasan, who was eighteen years my senior, and then my sister, Nalini Raghuram, eight years older than me. I'd always joke that they should actually have called me "Oops Haasan". I was not planned at all,' says Kamal Haasan with a laugh.

'But what happens when you come so late is that there is no sibling rivalry as such, instead there was a lot of fostering. Also because my father D. Srinivasan was in the Independence movement, I was sort of stuck in the era as if I had lived during that time. My siblings were all born before Independence, my sister was born in 1947. We were so proud of the new, independent India. I rejoiced with my father and my brothers; their positive attitude, their dreams of India were contagious. Of course, my father then became disenchanted and didn't get into active electoral politics. He moved away because he thought his job was done. So, the spirit of this child, was actually that of pre-Independence, and then of a new, independent India,' he says.

Kamal Haasan grew up cradled between the influences of a new India and the rise of the Dravidian movement against upper-caste Brahmin hegemony and to uphold a separate Dravidian identity and culture of the southern states. The movement was spearheaded by E.V. Ramasamy, popularly known as Periyar.[†]

[†] Periyar was a prominent social reformer, founder of the Self-Respect Movement for Tamils and then the political party Dravidar Kazhagam (DK). Considered the father of modern Tamil Nadu, both the DMK and

'Even though my father wasn't politically active, he had close ties to the Congress party. State leaders like K. Kamaraj [three-time Tamil Nadu chief minister and former Congress president] visited our home and we visited them. As a young boy, I listened to my father and his friends talk about politics; the rise of the DMK at that time was looked upon with both great chagrin and admiration at the same time. Later, when my elder brother Charuhasan became a DMK lawyer, my father and he stopped sitting together at dinner during the elections.'

'I thought politics should be avoided at the dinner table,' I say, laughing.

'Yes,' he smiles, 'but in our case, it may have ended badly so they studiously avoided sitting together. However, I got to hear both sides of the conversation. My eldest brother was an atheist while my other brother, Chandra Hasan, was a strong believer. But even though I was a mantra-chanting Brahmin boy till I was twelve, my atheist brother never heckled me for it. He just looked the other way. So, I was influenced by all of them. When I was seven or eight years old, I was very religious. I would spend two hours in the puja room every day. If you walked on the road outside my house in Chennai early in the morning, you would hear my shrill voice reciting Sanskrit mantras. However, those were volatile times. The rise of the Dravidian movement affected everyone, including those who were opposed to it.'

'How did the movement influence you?' I ask, wondering what changed this little boy's strong belief into staunch atheism.

'By the time I was twelve, what started off as doubt about religion totally swung to the other side of the spectrum, ably assisted by my elder brother. By sixteen, I was a borderline rabid atheist. Then, things cooled down, and I decided not to be angry. I finally settled down for a rational view of the world because for me it was not necessary to demolish God. However, the trigger point was the apathy I was seeing towards casteism around me.'

---

the All India Anna Dravida Munnetra Kazhagam (AIADMK) today claim to be followers of Periyar's principles.

The young boy had been brought up completely differently.

'For me, as I grew up, caste was like a car model, that's all,' he says. 'There was no derision or untouchability involved with it. Our house was an open house where many people came—it was not a typical Brahmin house—and when I was a young boy I had secretly become a non-vegetarian. When my mother found out, it was like finding out your son smokes. It was considered equally bad. However, when she would throw a five-rupee note at me, I knew what she meant. It was her way of telling me to go get my meat fix but not to tell her about it.

'I had started visiting Kerala with friends when I was sixteen years old. The political climate there was very similar to the Dravidian movement in Tamil Nadu. But it was better because being a bhakt in Kerala is possible, while being a staunch atheist is also possible. Those trips had a strong influence on me. When I was around eighteen, I finally realized that I was clearly not right wing at all.'

Kamal Haasan's early heroes were all individualistic mavericks. They appealed to him despite their iconic status. But he'd made it a point to question even those elevated to the status of idols—from Periyar to Mahatma Gandhi—in the Indian imagination.

'Periyar was one of the leaders who took on questions directly,' Kamal says. 'People would call him all kinds of names, he would quietly take it and give them a fitting answer, very much like Gandhiji. When I was eighteen, I was in a circle of people which was prone to Gandhi-bashing. However, at twenty-four, I discovered Mr Mohandas Karamchand Gandhi, with all his blemishes and pockmarks. Suddenly, his critics didn't matter to me any longer. I accepted him with all my heart, and he became my hero. If I had continued being a believer, I would have been a Gandhi bhakt. Fortunately, I was able to enjoy what he probably meant people to enjoy of him, his tenacity of purpose.'

Kamal Haasan's acting career unfolded virtually simultaneously with his informal political baptism. At just four years old, he debuted in the film *Kalathur Kannamma* for which he won the President's Gold Medal. Interestingly, Tamil films and the film industry were extremely political as opposed to the sanitized Hindi film industry. For example, former DMK chief minister M. Karunanidhi's fiery scripts and former AIADMK chief minister M.G. Ramachandran's hard-hitting roles were both key ingredients of their political journeys.

'You were in films from a very early age, how did that impact you?' I ask.

'The Tamil film industry was the most politicized film industry you could find,' he replies. 'People wondered why I wasn't politically influenced earlier on. I viewed the existing politics and politicians with derision because none of them kept their promises; they lied. There was no dedication. In any field, even cinema, I don't respect people who don't dedicate themselves to their work, people who are content living off the spoils. Also, it was a common thing to blame everything on politicians. However, at the time I was also discovering Gandhiji, and getting more and more close to him, despite disagreeing with some of the things he said. I came to a conclusion that Gandhiji is not impossible, he is imitable, he is not inimitable Gandhi. That's why I never call him Mahatma—the purpose of his life, the message is that he is *imitable* and not beyond the reach of a person with a will. We need to think about Gandhiji as a direction to life, not the way itself. It is *you* who has to figure out your life's purpose. But he is a good guide to have in mind. That's how people read the Bhagavad Gita, but I read another man, Gandhiji. It has been helpful to me and it is at that time my anger subsided and my commitment to society became stronger,' he says.

'How did this commitment, in a sense a political awakening, reflect in your film choices where you were always portrayed as a passionate and romantic hero?' I ask.

'Gandhiji himself was a passionate man, though we never heard that part of the story from Kasturbaji,' he says with a laugh. 'I am very sure he would have had great romance in him. Somewhere it is considered blasphemy to talk about Gandhiji's romance, but if you just translate it into romance for the country, it is acceptable. He himself willingly hung this brahmachari placard around his neck

which I didn't care for—those are the differences I had. My other
hero, Mr Periyar, married when he was in his sixties and people were
shocked at the time. But he had a very simple answer. He said, "I
needed it, I'm glad I'm still capable." These are my kind of heroes. So,
my romantic image was just another expression of myself, my beliefs,
one of the nine rasas we have of our art forms,' he says, smiling.

Gradually, however, Kamal Haasan's films became more
political. His 'dialogue with the people' started with the film *Hey
Ram* in 2000. The movie was written, produced, directed by and
starred Kamal Haasan as a man who wanted to assassinate Mahatma
Gandhi but is finally convinced of his beliefs, even though it's too
late to stop his killing.

Blunt as ever, he continues, 'You can see the route I took to
Gandhi. The counterargument to Gandhi was where I started. I
wanted to do it convincingly, because Gandhi's success is that he
took on the dialogue with those who opposed him and he won the
argument. I wanted my film to be convincing to the audience. Some
viewers thought the film was interesting but asked me, "Why did you
have to kill Gandhi in the end?" To an audience, a film story has no
commitment to history. That is, I think, belated psychotherapy on
what could have been but that doesn't work for me.'

'You question all your heroes, you question every idol you've
had. What were your questions about Gandhi?' I ask.

'The questions were not my own,' he replies. 'They were
questions I had heard about from other people, even from some of
the politicians I met. A senior politician from West Bengal once told
me, "I can understand why you like Gandhiji so much. It's because
he was also an actor like you." That's their way of putting him down.
Some of my communist friends say that the biggest street theatre was
when Gandhi enacted the Dandi March. These observations made
me laugh. They were not wrong. But so what if they were right? Did
it tarnish Gandhiji's character, did it take away from the message of
his life? It didn't. If you say the Dandi March was the biggest street

theatre performed, I'd say okay, but what is politics if not a form of theatre? What is a symbolic act but theatre? The whole idea of ahimsa itself seems theatrical, till you're ready for it. Not all are ready because it takes some time to truly be able to practise non-violence because the height of valour is ahimsa. How many people have that kind of valour, the bravery, to go that far? That's why the greatest Jain saint was called Mahavir. It's something to do with valour, to be so calm and so harmless towards everything. It's beyond religion, it's compassion and humanity in one word.'

After fifty years in the film industry, four National Awards and many other accolades, Kamal Haasan had in a sense reached his peak of superstardom in Tamil Nadu. And then came *Vishwaroop* in 2013 and his clash with the Tamil Nadu chief minister, Jayalalithaa, whom he describes as 'empress'.

'You've described your life today as the "unmaking of an actor and the making of a politician". Why leave a world you've literally been born into to enter a world of uncertainty?'

'When I came into the cinema business, success wasn't assured either,' he replies. 'But I came into it with a purpose. I just wanted to be in the best cinema which could be enjoyed by people and make them happy, that's all. It was a simple ambition but very hard to achieve given the pressures of business and the industry. They can do cosmetic surgery on anything and ruin the whole character so I've been fighting that, taking all the risks possible. I will do the same here.'

'The biggest risk of course was your clash with Jayalalithaa in 2013, when you had, in a sense, everything to lose?' I interject.

'Yes, in a sense, I had been hounded for a long time,' he says. 'I didn't realize it then but some people from the acting business kept sidelining me unfairly. Any new act I did would be ridiculed first and then accepted after the people liked it. So, I thought it was a way of life for me. Politicians didn't understand where I was heading. In *Hey Ram*, they saw a poster of a man with a sacred thread holding a gun and constructed a whole story against me. I truly feared that the story of *Hey*

Ram would one day happen in reality, that religion would justify this taking up the gun. In *Hey Ram*, an impending sense of disaster and fear were there but equally there were counterarguments against this. Even today, against religious violence there are equally strong people raising voices and I'm glad India still has such spirit,' he says.

'All my films were interfered in from then on,' he continues. 'I really thought politicians simply didn't like me.'

Then came *Vishwaroop*, one of Kamal Haasan's most ambitious films made in 2013 which has a Muslim protagonist. He plays a RAW officer who infiltrates an Al Qaeda network undercover.

'For *Vishwaroop*, it was complicated in a sense. Jaya TV, which was owned by Chief Minister Jayalalithaa, bid for the rights to my film. It was a direct business so I couldn't say no to the highest bid; it was a deal with the chief minister. They made an offer I couldn't refuse, however, then came the other offer,' he says, hinting at an illegal offer of payment. 'It became very complicated. Everyone knows that I don't touch black money. I don't accept it at all, so then there was this discussion, that was also sorted, when I said you must understand, I won't take it. It's no personal affront but I could not. I think she took umbrage at anyone refusing an offer one cannot afford to refuse. She miscalculated what I could afford and how far I would go to defend my self-respect.

'Then, two people were sent to see my film. One of them was the police chief of Tamil Nadu who was very close to the chief minister. The other was the head of Jaya TV, who was later fired. They went back and reported that the film could cause trouble. So, the police chief turned into the censor chief. It was a complete breakdown of democracy,' he says.

However, *Vishwaroop* was cleared by the Censor Board and Kamal Haasan began preparing for the film release on various platforms. And then the state banned the film on the grounds that it would create 'law-and-order problems'.

'What I think happened,' he muses, 'is that after a certain time it became personal. How dare I? She banned the film and expected me to go grovelling and begging because that's what people advised me to do. When my film was banned, the whole industry came and it was like a funeral in my office, everyone sitting with a sad face.'

The protests against the film by Muslim groups in Tamil Nadu was a false protest, orchestrated politically.

'They created a league of concerned Muslim gentlemen. The irony was that the only good guy in the film, the hero of *Vishwaroop*, was an Indian Muslim. I couldn't understand why anyone would take umbrage because my idea wasn't to lose one section of an audience. I'm not a RSS guy with an ideology. I was just an entertainer, I had made a film like, say, *Amar Akbar Anthony*; you make a film to please all communities. I wanted everyone to come to the theatre.'

With a 'tenacity of purpose', Kamal Haasan continued to fight for his film. He showed it to different Muslim groups in Mumbai, who also didn't understand why objections had been raised. He met film associations to appeal for their support and took the ban to court.

'We then cleared the ban through the courts and a premiere was planned in Los Angeles. On my way to LA, I received a call from my brother through the pilot. He told me that they had banned my film again!'

Kamal Haasan pauses, reliving the tension of that time as I say, laughingly, 'They must have waited till they knew you were mid-air, so there was nothing you could do.'

'I was literally in limbo,' he says, laughing. 'When I landed, my return tickets were ready. Then I made a call which changed my life forever. Enough was enough. I said we are releasing the film in Los Angeles. You can't do this to an individual, especially not an artiste. So, I released it there and back in India. Some of the states neighbouring Tamil Nadu also released it.'

However, because of the ban in Tamil Nadu, some other places with a large Muslim population, like Malaysia and Dubai, also banned the film, so he was still in a limbo as he describes it.

Again, Kamal Haasan was advised to just apologize to the chief minister. Again, he refused.

'I said I am not, I will not, and if I go down, I will go down with this film. By then my financier had probably been advised—no financier takes that kind of action—but he wanted all the money I had borrowed from him, repaid before the film's release. I still had to sell the film at the time, so I signed a document which said if you don't pay up, I am going to confiscate all your property.'

'So, you basically signed away your house, your office, your property, everything?' I say.

'Everything, everything,' he says emphatically. 'All immovable property that I owned belonged to him. So, I signed it and then went back to court again. And we won. And I paid back the man. That's when I said that if the film is not released, if they keep on hounding me, I'll find another state or country that is democratic, if need be. It was Hussain first, then it'll be Haasan.'

It would have been a repeat of another artiste being hounded out of India but he says, 'They made it sound like Haasan was whining and crying and the Empress came and said, "Kamal Haasan is a fifty-eight-year-old man, he's not a child, he knows what he's invested and if someone takes away his money, that's part of business. What can the government do about that? We have only this amount of police force and this film will create a riot that the police force can't handle." That's a fantastic route for Article 356, by the way,' he adds. 'If you can't handle law and order, let the Centre handle it but I was too tired at that point of time to take it up. This was the case and I stood my ground.'

'Did you ever meet Jayalalithaa?' I ask.

'After all this we never met; there was no meeting at all,' he says tersely. 'I lost Rs 60 crore over this tussle with *Vishwaroop* and I thought it was worth it. I had said when I get Rs 1 lakh per film, I'll do one film at a time—that was about twenty-five–thirty years ago. I've been paid 200, 300, now it's thousand times more and much more than what I wanted, so everything is a bonus. But what I have, my honour and my pride, is worth much more. That's the time I became political. I kept on doing movies, I did not stop, but four years later it was only after her death that I was able to release *Vishwaroop 2.*'

'Did your family, your daughters, ever tell you to stop, that there's no point feuding with an all-powerful person, it's only a film?' I ask.

He stops and thinks before answering, 'You know, the kind of power anyone has to make me do that was only my brother Chandra Hasan. Strangely, midway during this tension, he told me, "I'm with you. It's your money, you've earned it. It's not squandering, that much I know, you're not throwing it away. You're making a bid for your honour. If you think it's worth it, I'm with you. But I'm angry." So, he is the one who went to court every day. These are tensions he didn't have to deal with at his age, but he was like a father to me. He kept telling me he will have to step away from my life if I become a politician, to which I used to smile. He used to ask me what was on my mind and I used to joke and say just like the chief minister even he wants to know what's in my mind. He also used to say, "I can't take the tension if you are in politics." I used to say we'll cross that bridge when we get there. Somehow, I think he was very sure that I would go in this direction because he was very close to me. He was the only man who could have stopped me then. The rest of the industry came, advised me, including Sivaji's son, who said she expects you to kneel, why don't you? I said I'm nearing sixty and my knees are stiff, they won't bend!'

Humorous even as he recounts his worse moments, there are also flashes of anger. 'So it was anger, even if it was in a positive sense, that drove you to politics?' I prod him.

'It was complete and righteous wrath,' he answers.

Surely the larger dilemma he will face is how does one translate wrath into a larger political vision. Comparisons are often made between Arvind Kejriwal, who attended the launch of his political party, Makkal Needhi Maiam (People's Justice Centre), and Kamal Haasan, both outsiders to traditional politics, which is in a sense both their biggest appeal and their biggest challenge. What will be the making of Kamal Haasan the politician?

'What will be the concrete vision you have beyond opposing someone or some party's politics?' I ask.

'If you come to Tamil Nadu, you see the traction with people,' he answers. 'I am the only politician who takes questions directly from the people. They are asking all kinds of questions and I am answering them. It is not only educative but it is encouraging for me because I have the answers to give them, and I'm honest enough to say if I have to look into something. I ask them to come and explain what they're looking for, make a policy with us. What we have now is people I truly respect sitting around a table with me, I'm not talking down to them, we're talking among equals, a lot of good minds, whom I didn't even know before, I didn't have a chance of meeting, and now they're part of the party.'

Describing his political motivations in particular, Kamal says he wanted to know what ails Tamil Nadu—the quickest answer would be to say corrupt politicians, but how did that happen? 'The inaction of people like *me*. All of us are armchair commentators—it should have happened this way, it could have happened this way. It is like the moment Godard and Truffaut came up with in the heady new wave cinema days, when they kept criticizing and making film-makers angry and they were thrown a challenge, "You keep talking, you're nothing but loudmouths, come and make a film and then you will know." And they did exactly that and they changed the face of French cinema,' he says.

Kamal Haasan compares his entry into politics with another much more well-known one.

'It's happened before in 1908 when Gandhiji returned and changed the character of the Congress party itself. And he was a funny-looking man, his dress sense wasn't accepted, he didn't look like a barrister and he didn't behave like a politician—he was too busy cleaning toilets. They really didn't understand the tangent on which he was travelling. Similarly here they've forgotten I have no inventions to make—it's all already there,' he says. 'Our Constitution is robust, we have great leaders who have great ideology. I'm a centrist and that's new. I believe in centrism. It's not inaction, it's acting at the right time. And then you have to lean to one side or the other. There's no shame in leaning to the right side, I don't just mean religion but in the right or wrong part of it.'

Where then does Kamal Haasan place himself in the all-India political picture? Neither right nor left. His party is contesting the 2019 elections. Does he see himself, a rationalist atheist, as a natural opponent to the BJP, and does that mean a closeness to the Congress or a strong regional party which will remain equidistant from the two poles of national politics?

'For me, I'm an Indian Tamilian. This moment it's not Swachh Bharat to me but Swachh Tamil Nadu. When I spoke at one of the meetings, there was this talk of how BJP will destroy Dravidian politics forever. But was our position that Dravidian politics has come to an end?' he asks. 'No, I raised my voice and some basic truths came out. Dravidianism isn't limited to Tamilians. Anthropologically speaking and politically speaking, Dravidianism is pan national. So you can't do away with the Dravidians or Dravidian politics.'

Indian, Tamilian, actor, politician, will Kamal Haasan succeed in his latest avatar? As we end, a parting shot from him, as I ask, 'Should the prime minister of our country take questions from people like you do?'

'Only if he has the answers,' he retorts. The last word of this round goes to Kamal Haasan.

[11]

Kailash Satyarthi

Giving India's Children Freedom

Kailash Satyarthi and my paths have crossed many times. I first interviewed him at the NDTV studio in Delhi when he was considered a maverick activist heading the NGO Bachpan Bachao Andolan. Back then, he had calmly challenged the then child welfare minister Krishna Tirath to accompany him to places in the national capital where children as young as eight years old slaved the whole day at illegal factories for a pittance. She had ignored the challenge despite his repeated attempts. Given the fearlessness with which he has taken on public figures, it's perhaps not surprising that he has never received an Indian government award, even though in 2014, Kailash Satyarthi was the first Indian to be awarded the Nobel Peace Prize for his relentless crusade for children's rights, an honour he shared with the young Pakistani activist Malala Yousafzai.[*]

---

[*] Interview conducted on 19 July 2018, New Delhi

His journey began in the small, dusty town of Vidisha in Madhya Pradesh. He was born into a traditional Brahmin family, the youngest of four brothers and a sister. But his family soon realized there was nothing traditional about this little boy at that time called Kailash Sharma.

'The very first day of school was an eye-opener for me,' Satyarthi reminisces. 'I was about five and half years old, on my way to school with my family, when I encountered a cobbler boy sitting with his father on the road. The boy was the same age as me. He was looking at our feet and not our faces. I felt disturbed. Why was a child sitting outside on the road, and not with the rest of us inside the classroom? When I asked my family members, they explained to me that it was not uncommon for poor children to help their families out with work. I wasn't convinced by the answer. Slowly, I gathered my courage, and one day, when I was coming back from school, I found the boy again. I stopped and asked the boy and his father why they didn't send him to school. The boy was shy, and the father was shocked. He apologized, saying that the thought had never occurred to him, because he belonged to a marginalized community and he came from a long line of cobblers. He felt that education was forbidden to people like them. His answer made me even more frustrated. I felt very upset and angry that some children had to live their lives assuming that they had to work because they were born to a particular caste.'

Kailash Sharma never forgot the incident. And as he grew up, he began to notice how 'untouchability' surrounded him everywhere—both at home and in the outside world.

'Even when the sweepers would come home to clean, they weren't allowed into our kitchens. Their food was just thrown into their buckets. Neither were they allowed into the nearby temple. It was then that I started looking at the world with different eyes, a different perspective. I started noticing other children on the streets, working in small workshops and restaurants, but I didn't know what to do and whom to talk to. It couldn't be possible that some children are born to work or that it was their destiny. And finally, I was convinced that one shouldn't believe everything that elders say. You should question situations. If you don't find the answers, then try to find the answer inside you, but you must keep on questioning the world around you. I did, and found that most accepted norms were biased, wrong and unjust.'

At fifteen, Satyarthi thought he had finally found the answers to his questions. In 1969, the country was celebrating Mahatma Gandhi's birth centenary. Politicians in white starched kurtas addressed huge rallies speaking against untouchability. The teenager was mesmerized by the fiery speeches and felt he had discovered his calling—politics.

'The leaders were addressing the masses and speaking against untouchability, so I was very impressed,' he says. 'I thought these people are genuinely better than my own family. I started dreaming of becoming a politician. So, I thought I'd organize something special. The idea was to invite women sweepers to cook food at a newly built Gandhi park in town and to invite local political leaders. They'd come and eat the food and it would, in turn, send a very deep message to the township—high-caste leaders are open to eating food cooked by sweepers.'

The determined teenager, with the help of a few friends, then organized a feast. On the day of the event, they waited for the VIP guests to arrive.

'Despite agreeing to attend the occasion, none of the leaders turned up,' he says. 'There were only five of us friends and six women and male sweepers. So, we ate the food. I came back home to find a gathering of people in our courtyard. There was tension in the air and I realized something was wrong. My mother was crying, my brothers were pleading with the priests who were part of the group. A few relatives were also there. The priests had announced that my family were now considered outcastes because of what I'd done.'

Even today the hurt and humiliation is fresh in Kailash Satyarthi's mind. 'I tried to convince them. I told them about all the political leaders who had spoken up against untouchability. This led to a heated argument. Finally, the priests concurred that for me and my family to stay within the caste, there was only one option. I would have to be taken to the Ganga for a *shuddhi*, or purification, ritual and then we would have to host a feast for Brahmins. That made me even angrier. I was already perturbed by the political hypocrisy and now it was directed at the religious and social hypocrisy I was witnessing first-hand. I refused to participate in the rituals. So, it was decided that at home, I would be given a separate room with a door which opened on to the street. In other words, I had become an untouchable in my own family.' He pauses. 'It's easy to talk about it now but at that time I was shattered. I was the youngest in the family and pampered a lot. I'd always sit with my mother and eat, and she would never eat without me. But from that day onwards, I was served food and water in a separate thali. The pressures of society and family were so strong that they simply couldn't avoid it. So, I lived like that for several years in my room.'

It shocks me to hear that his exile lasted so long. I would've thought that it would've lasted a few days at the most.

'*Nahi nahi,*' he replies. 'For several years! Sometimes my mother would come and pick up the food from the plate and put it my mouth to feed me, crying all the time. But I wasn't allowed into the kitchen. On the day of the incident, I remember thinking—who are they to cast me out? I will cast out the whole caste system! My surname, Sharma, was my caste name; it identified me as a Brahmin, so I decided to give myself a new name.

'Legally, I couldn't change my name till I was eighteen. So, the day I turned eighteen, I chose my new name. Satyarthi means "seeker of truth", and it doesn't represent any caste. People are often confused and cannot tell if I am I a Dalit, Harijan or Buddhist. I leave them to their own assumptions.' He smiles.

Life went on for the newly christened Satyarthi. He studied engineering according to his parents' wishes, and briefly taught at the Samrat Ashok Technological Institute, Vidisha, Bhopal University. The issue of children remained close to his heart but all he did was write articles about it in newspapers. In 1978, he married a girl from Delhi, Sumedha, and with help from her and her family, he decided to start his own magazine called *Sangharsh Jari Rahega*. But his life was soon about to change.

'One day, a stranger knocked on my door. His name was Wasal Khan and he was carrying an old copy of my magazine. He asked me if this was the place where the magazine was produced. When I asked him to come in, he fell on the floor, unconscious.

'Wasal Khan was sick and had been hungry for a few days. He had been knocking on every possible door and finally got to know about me through a subscriber of my magazine in Chandigarh. He was a desperate father whose daughter was about to be sold to a brothel,' Satyarthi says. 'And as a journalist, I began recording his story.'

It was Wasal Khan's story which began the transition of Kailash Satyarthi from journalist to activist.

'His only expectation was that I'd write about his saga and that he could finally get justice for his daughter. As he spoke, more chilling details emerged. For the first time, I heard of intergenerational slavery. He told me that he and his newly married wife, along with a few other families, were lured away from his native village in Aligarh. They were taken to work at a brick kiln in Punjab near the Sirhind area. For seventeen years they were confined there. They couldn't leave, and life was hell. Wasal Khan grew old and was resigned to the fact that he'd die there.

'Then one day, his wife noticed that a few people had arrived to negotiate a deal . . . a deal to buy their fifteen-year-old daughter. The strangers who'd arrived at the site were brothel owners. They were ready to pay a certain amount of money for the girl, but the "owners" of Wasal Khan and his family wanted more. As they negotiated, they'd touch and prod the girl's body while the mother watched silently. Wasal Khan's daughter was their hope for the future; they didn't want her to become a slave like them. Wasal Khan's wife begged him to save their daughter. He was at a loss. That night, he sneaked into a brick-loaded truck without knowing where the truck was going. At Chandigarh, he got off and pleaded to anyone who'd listen to him for help. And somehow he found his way to me,' says Satyarthi.

But as Kailash Satyarthi listened to Wasal Khan's story, he put down his pen.

'I began to think . . .' he says. 'What if she were my daughter? What would I do then? I wouldn't just write about it and wait and hope for people to give it attention and the government to act on it? So, I told Wasal Khan that I wasn't going to write anything. Instead, I was going to rescue his daughter.

'Wasal was startled and immediately protested, saying we would all be brutally attacked. But I insisted and nothing was going to change my mind. So, I started thinking about the next step. I called a few friends for help. I asked Sumedha, my wife, to sell her wedding ornaments so that we could organize a truck since Wasal had informed me that there were around thirty to forty people who were held in bondage. We made all the arrangements and soon set off for Punjab.

It all happened exactly as Wasal had warned, Kailash Satyarthi remembers wryly.

'We arrived at the brick kiln in Punjab where he had worked, he was caught in front of us by the owners and their goons, we were beaten up, clothes torn, and barefooted we ran for miles because the truck we took with us, the driver ran away because he was also frightened. Somehow, we reached Delhi, beaten, but not wiser. The only option I had left was the judiciary. I spoke to a few friends who were lawyers and they informed me that there was no law against child labour in India. However, there was an old British law which was never ever used, the habeas corpus provision.[†] Under this provision, we could ask for the children to be presented in court and we did exactly that.'

On 22 March 1981, a landmark day, for the first time one man's private effort led to the exposure of modern-day slavery in independent India.[‡] With the help of the court, Kailash Satyarthi was able to free thirty-six children, women and men from bonded labour in Punjab.

'The Delhi High court freed them under habeas corpus, and not a child labour law because none existed yet,' Satyarthi says. 'Yet, it was a milestone for Indian children and me. This laid the ground for transformative legislation for India's children.

'It was also a personal turning point for me. Freeing those children, talking to the fifteen-year-olds, holding their hands from the High Court to my small office near Mandi House. They had never seen cars or such big buildings and roads, so they were jumping around like monkeys. I was watching them carefully, and suddenly it struck me—I had not freed them; it was *they* who had freed me. I had heard of liberty, liberation, moksha, mukti, independence and

---

[†] Habeas corpus is a law that states that a person cannot be kept in prison unless they have first been brought before a court of law, which decides whether it is legal for them to be kept in prison.

[‡] https://www.livemint.com/Leisure/ehtcRH1tQB1GsSDhha7nbJ/Kailash-Satyarthi-The-child-rights-champion.html

all kinds of things but this was true freedom. I saw God here in those children, and this had now become my way of worship,' he says, his voice filled with passion.

After this victory, Kailash Satyarthi began getting calls from all over India, from the stone quarries of Haryana, to Maharashtra, to Madhya Pradesh, where women, men, children were being held as bonded labour.

'The whole country became aware about slavery in India and that we could no longer ignore it. Child slavery is the worst because children have no voice to speak for themselves. They are the most vulnerable to sexual abuse and trafficking. "Trafficking", "bonded labour" and "slavery"—these terms were not properly understood in India back then. In fact, even globally, trafficking wasn't seen as an issue for many years.

'We had to fight for six years for an anti–child labour law. There were a few provisions in the old British laws, which could be used. For example, children couldn't be employed in the mining industry. But no one considered child labour a serious problem. Child labour is not simply about poverty; it is a denial of human and child rights. For instance, in the 1980s, I exposed the thousands of children working in the carpet industries in Mirzapur in Uttar Pradesh, the government agencies denied this completely. Two prime ministers, Indira Gandhi and then Chandra Shekhar, spoke in Parliament saying there were forces trying to defame India, when India was organizing the Commonwealth Games. This was in reference to me because the world media had started pressuring international buyers not to buy carpets made in India because of child labour. In a sense, what I was doing made me an anti-national,' he says sombrely. 'However, the judicial interventions from 1986, when the first anti–child labour law (The Child Labour [Prohibition and Regulation] Act, 1986) was enacted, have been the strongest support against child labour and slavery.'

So, with the judiciary backing him, Kailash Satyarthi kept fighting what seemed a lone battle, with the police, state governments and even the media ignoring his crusade.

The rest, as they say, is history. Kailash Satyarthi's journey from being an outcaste in his own family to an anti-national and then a Nobel Peace Laureate is an incredible one.

Kailash Satyarthi laughs as he recollects that day when the award was announced. 'On 10 October 2014, I got a call from a journalist, Saurabh, from NDTV. I was on my computer looking for cheap tickets to Germany where I had been invited to speak at an event; I felt that the organizers shouldn't have to pay too much for my tickets, so I was trying to figure out the cheapest fare. All Saurabh could manage on the phone were the words "Nobel Prize". He was so excited that he couldn't even finish the sentence. At first, I thought it was someone like Sri Sri Ravi Shankar or the prime minister of India who had received it and they wanted my reaction. In the meantime, my colleagues and my son burst into the room, crying tears of joy. It was only when I looked at the official Nobel website that I believed it.'

I remember that day clearly as well. In our newsroom, I had asked if it was the same persistent man who wouldn't let the minister get away with her vague replies. That day, as people googled to find out who Kailash Satyarthi was, I felt a moment of pride. Here was a man who just wouldn't give up speaking for those who had no voice.

'What has the Nobel Prize meant to you?' I ask.

'It was a defining moment for me and for India. It was the first time an Indian had received a Nobel Prize for Peace. But most importantly, it was a defining moment for the millions of children whom we rescued, and who, in turn, in the truest sense of the word, had rescued me . . . by giving me the ultimate freedom.'

In his Nobel acceptance speech, Kailash Satyarthi summed up his vision eloquently. He said:

'I refuse to accept that the shackles of slavery can ever be stronger than the quest for freedom. I refuse to accept that all the temples and mosques and churches and prayer houses have no place for the dreams of our children. I challenge the passivity and pessimism surrounding our children. I challenge this culture of silence, this culture of neutrality.'

At sixty-five, Kailash Satyarthi remains a challenger—the challenger of the status quo regarding India's children.

[12]

Fali Nariman

Justice, as a Client

The grand old man of Indian jurisprudence, ninety-year-old Fali Nariman still makes it a point to go to the Supreme Court every day. Charming, with a twinkle in his eye, he offers me chocolates as we settle down in his home to talk about the defining moments—glorious and ignominious—in India's legal story. Who better, after all, to discuss this with than a man who started as a young lawyer at the Mumbai bar, sixty-nine years ago in November 1950? Even today, his command of constitutional law and legal acumen puts many younger lawyers to shame.[*]

[*] Interview conducted on 28 July 2018, New Delhi

'My client, my lord, is the independence of the judiciary.'
It was with these dramatic words that Fali Nariman stood up in the Supreme Court in 2015 to argue against what he considered an existential threat to the integrity of the judiciary.

In his sitting room, with family photographs scattered around, including those of his wife of sixty-four years, Bapsi, and son, Supreme Court justice Rohinton Nariman, Fali Nariman describes to me the events that led to this dramatic denouement, remarkably recalling each key date.

'In May 2014, the new NDA government took charge. A few months later, in August 2014, it introduced the Constitution 121st Amendment Bill No: 97 of 2014 in the Lok Sabha as well as the National Judicial Appointments Commission [NJAC]† Bill 96 of 2014 along the lines of the bills of the predecessor government giving primacy in the ultimate selection of judges in the higher judiciary to non-judges. The two bills were then passed with near unanimity in both the Lok Sabha and the Rajya Sabha and submitted to the President of India for his assent.

'The constitutional challenge to these bills/acts was then fixed for hearing before the Constitution bench of five judges on Wednesday, 15 April 2015. Importantly, however, since there had been no interim stay granted by the court, the government decided to go ahead by bringing in these sweeping legislative and constitutional measures,' narrates Nariman.

This was crucial. With no stay given by the Supreme Court, it meant that even while the case against this NJAC—which was to be

---

† https://indiankanoon.org/doc/66970168/

headed by the chief justice of India (CJI) as chairman—was being argued, the process was being put into motion for it to begin work by the government.

'That was exactly the point,' exclaims Fali. 'They wanted to bring in a fait accompli. On 13 April 2015, the Central government issued a gazette notification which would bring into force this new commission now meant to authoritatively recommend the appointments of all Supreme and High Court judges. This included the CJI as chairman, along with two of the senior-most judges of the Supreme Court of India as members, the law minister but with two additional persons described in the Act as "eminent persons". This new system of appointments would replace the then prevailing "collegium" system (consisting wholly of five senior-most judges of the Supreme Court of India), which recommended all appointments to the higher judiciary. The collegium system had been brought into effect by a larger bench of nine judges way back in 1993—further fine-tuned by another bench of nine judges in 1995.'

Fali Nariman, and many others, were worried that the phrasing 'eminent persons' in this new commission was loaded and vague enough to include anyone of the current government's choice. And it was loaded because any two members of the commission could veto the recommendations of the six-member commission! The scale of balance in this new NJAC would therefore be effectively tilted towards the executive. The government and others, however, argued that the current collegium system, which consisted of the CJI and the four senior-most judges of the Supreme Court, had created an 'empire within an empire' with a lack of transparency and no oversight over judicial appointments.

'It was an insidious attempt by the government to fill the judiciary with its cronies,' says Fali Nariman, 'and that's why I opposed this Appointments Commission.'

'We were arguing the case and at that point we didn't get a stay. We were frothing at our mouths because while this matter went on and on in court, the commission could simultaneously fill all the vacancies and then it would be too late if they began appointments.'

'The government was in such a hurry to implement this,' he remembers, 'that over the weekend a meeting was called by the Prime Minister's Office to consider the names of persons to be appointed for the vacancies, including the names of two "eminent persons", so that the commission could be constituted and start functioning.'

It was at this stage, in Fali's view, that the supreme defining moment came.

'Irrespective of the outcome of the challenge already pending in court to the constitutional and legislative acts passed by Parliament, the CJI in his wisdom wrote a letter to Prime Minister Modi stating his inability to participate as chairman of the NJAC. Chief Justice Dattu wrote that it was inappropriate for him to function as chairman of the proposed commission when a challenge to the constitutional validity of the statute itself was pending before a Constitution bench of his court—the Supreme Court of India. This letter was read out in open court, and severely criticized by the then attorney general of India Mukul Rohatgi appearing for the Union of India in the fourth week of April 2015.'

That was the turning point in the case, a relieved Fali Nariman tells me.

'Ultimately, after a hearing and much argument, a divided court, headed by Honourable Justice J.S. Khehar, handed down in October 2015 its majority decision of four judges to one, striking down both the constitutional amendment as well as the NJAC Act. What was important was the presence of mind shown by the then CJI and his resolve to uphold the independence and integrity not only of the office of the CJI but of the institution of the Supreme Court of India by refusing to participate in the proceedings of the NJAC until the final decision of the cases pending in court.'

More importantly, this vindicated Fali Nariman's determination to fight this case tooth and nail, appearing personally in every hearing, with the legal might of the government against him.

'It's a judgment which has preserved the independence of our judiciary for our future generations and will continue to do so. Otherwise it would have been impossible to live in this country without freedom for our judiciary to function,' he says. 'That's why I had to take up this fight.'

Explaining the full context, he adds, 'To understand the significance of what happened, a little background is necessary. On 10 July 2013, when the UPA government was in power, two separate judgments on two separate cases by a bench of the Supreme Court of India were handed down. In one of them (in the case of Lily Thomas),[‡] the court held invalid and unconstitutional the provisions of Section 8(4) of the Representation of People Act, 1951. As a consequence, all members of Parliament and members of state legislatures no longer enjoyed the special privilege that had been conferred on them since 1951. The privilege was—to be treated differently from all other persons convicted of offences and sentenced to imprisonment for terms in excess of two years. So, under the Representation of People Act, 1951 members of Parliament and members of the Legislative Assembly [MLAs] who stood convicted of offences involving imprisonment for terms of two years and upwards could not be disqualified if a stay had been obtained from a higher court. But with the striking down of Section 8(4) this special privilege for MPs and MLAs was denied and they were treated just as any other citizen.

'Similarly, in the other case, the Supreme Court of India upheld an order of the High Court of Patna declaring that a person who was confined in prison had no right to vote[§] by virtue of the provisions

---

[‡]   https://lawbriefs.in/706-lily-thomas-vs-union-of-india/

[§]   https://www.livelaw.in/allahabad-hc-upholds-validity-representation-peoples-act-2013-amendment/

contained in Section 62(2) of the Representation of People Act, 1951. Since he/she was not an "elector", they were therefore not qualified to contest elections to either house of Parliament or to the legislative assembly of a state.

'These two judgments,' Fali Nariman says, 'did not go down well with the representatives of the people in Parliament. There was universal antipathy in the corridors of power to the two judgments of the Supreme Court of India and what followed in the coming days was significant.

'The introduction of four separate bills meant to nullify the two Supreme Court judgments and introduce a constitutional amendment and a law regarding appointment of judges with a NJAC. Ironically, it was these two bills introduced by the Manmohan Singh government that were carried over by the successor Modi government and made law!'

So, in attempting to gain political control over the judiciary, both the UPA and NDA have shared a common cause. No wonder Finance Minister Arun Jaitley condemned the Supreme Court judgment striking down the NJAC by saying, 'Indian democracy cannot be a tyranny of the unelected'.

However, Fali Nariman has never been concerned with which government is in power. All that matters to him are his principles. In fact, during the Emergency of June 1975, he was among the few people who resigned from his government position in protest.

'Those were extraordinary circumstances and extraordinary times,' I say.

'Yes,' he says. 'I was additional solicitor general from May 1972 to June 1975. Since I was one of the main legal officers of the Indira Gandhi government, I could no longer support the government legally in defending the Emergency and so I resigned. I remember the then attorney general had cried when I met him. He told me how he wished he too could resign. But his wife was Swedish, and he was afraid that she might get arrested. We all had that fear back then. I was afraid I could have been arrested. However, nothing happened,' he remembers with a smile. 'In fact, Mrs Gandhi wrote me a nice letter accepting my resignation, saying that I had done a good job during my term of office.

'Bruce Grant, the Australian High Commissioner at the time, and I would go for a walk together in Nehru Park,' Nariman continues. 'He told me that one week after the declaration of Emergency, Mrs Gandhi had said to him that she was absolutely surprised at how the intellectuals had behaved in this country. She had expected much more agitation, when in fact there was none!

'My resignation wasn't reported anywhere in the Indian press. People in India only found out about it when the *New York Times* had reported it. In fact, some judges came to my residence and told me how foolish it was of me taking a stand no one knew about. There are different ways of looking at different things,' he says with a smile.

Throughout his legal career, Fali Nariman has always stood up for what he believes. The tragedy of the Emergency, he says, was that the highest judiciary didn't do the same, except for a few men and women.

'It's in critical times that individual men and women matter. In 1976, I remember the landmark ADM Jabalpur vs Shiv Kant Shukla case' which came to be known popularly as the habeas corpus case ["Habeas corpus" meant: "Thou shall have the body in Court"** and such cases are usually used to challenge illegal detentions by governments], where those detained during the Emergency went to court against their arrests. The detainees were represented by Shanti Bhushan, Ram Jethmalani, and Soli Sorabjee, among others, and the Government was represented by Attorney General Niren De. The latter famously argued that the arguments of detainees were illegal as all fundamental rights, even Article 21 of the Constitution, were

---

'   https://indiankanoon.org/doc/1735815/
** Oxford Dictionaries (1973), vol. I, p. 909.

suspended during the Emergency. Justice H.R. Khanna had asked, "Article 21 deals with life. Would the government's arguments extend to it also?"[††] The attorney general replied, "Even if life was to be taken illegally during the Emergency, the courts are helpless.'"

'What Justice H.R. Khanna did at the time was truly extraordinary,' Fali Nariman continues. 'He wasn't half as distinguished as many of his peers at that time, yet these were the judges who, when the time came, failed us. Justice H.R. Khanna was second in seniority and expected to be the next CJI. Even though he had the most to lose, he was the only dissenting voice amongst his four fellow judges.'

In their final judgment, the CJI and three other Supreme Court judges went against the judgments of nine high courts and held that no citizen had the right to move the courts against the legality of their detention in view of the Presidential Order declaring the Emergency. The lone voice opposing was Justice H.R. Khanna's.[‡‡]

'The Supreme Court as a body had abjectly failed in its duty, yet this was Justice Khanna's finest hour,' Fali Nariman says. 'In his eloquently written judgment, Justice H. R. Khanna observed, "The principle that no one shall be deprived of his life and liberty without the authority of law was not the gift of the Constitution. Thus, even in the absence of Article 21, the state does not hold any power to deprive the citizens of their right to liberty."

'Justice H.R. Khanna paid the price for this because when the time came for him to be appointed chief justice, another junior judge, Justice Beg, was recommended to the government by the CJI— and appointed. This became known as the "Second Supersession". Justice Khanna knew this would happen, yet he still did what he had to do. "There should be a statue to commemorate this great man and what he did," wrote the *New York Times* (contemporaneously).

[††] http://delhihighcourt.nic.in/annualreport_2007_2008
[‡‡] https://www.firstpost.com/india/43-years-since-emergency-a-look-back-at-hr-khanna-the-judge-who-stood-up-to-indira-gandhi-365539.html

'In fact,' Nariman continues, 'recently, a student came up to me and asked me an interesting question. When a practising priest, Yogi Adityanath, was appointed as chief minister of India's largest and most populist state in Uttar Pradesh in 2017, I had publicly declared that we are becoming a Hindu State. The student asked me why I would think that, especially when we have our basic structure doctrine that doesn't allow any change in the fundamental structure of our Constitution.[§§] "But you see," I said, "this is decided not by God but by women and men. Who knows what they will do? If a majoritarian government gets enough votes, they can say: to hell with your basic structure, we want this changed. That is why I maintain that even though we have our faults and our difficulties, the majoritarian government is still not something to be desired for a country as diverse as India.'

'Majoritarian' is an interesting word to use. 'Do you mean religious or political majoritarianism?' I ask.

'This is nothing to do with the Congress and the BJP; they are all on the same level,' he says. 'The public look up to the judiciary as supreme interpreters of the Constitution. It is the Supreme Court which laid down the basic structure doctrine of the Constitution. The majoritarian government at the time of Emergency [the Congress] was attempting to make new laws which were unchangeable; and they were putting them in the ninth schedule of the Constitution,

---

[§§] On April 24, 1973, the Supreme Court of India declared that Parliament did not have the power to amend certain aspects of the Constitution, its 'basic structure'. The Constitution empowers the Parliament and the state legislatures to make laws within their respective jurisdiction. Bills to amend the Constitution can only be introduced in the Parliament, but this power is not absolute. If the Supreme Court finds any law made by the Parliament inconsistent with the Constitution, it has the power to declare that law to be invalid. Thus, to preserve the ideals and philosophy of the original Constitution, the Supreme Court has laid down the basic structure doctrine. According to the doctrine, the Parliament cannot destroy or alter the basic structure of the doctrine.

making them unchallengeable in court. This included a law that said action against the press could not be challenged. That was the wish of the then majoritarian government.

'In 2015, as well, during this present majoritarian government, they were trying to push the NJAC through so they could gain control over the judiciary. That is why we must maintain the independence of the judiciary at all costs,' he says.

At ninety, Fali Nariman is fighting to keep the flag of an independent judiciary flying high. Safeguarding the Constitution is still his ultimate raison d'être.

[13]

Kiran Mazumdar-Shaw

A Woman Who Means Business

The smiling and confident sixty-five-year-old chairperson and managing director of Biocon Limited, India's largest biopharmaceutical company, has many firsts to her name. From a business that started in a Bangalore garage, today Kiran Mazumdar-Shaw, a first-generation entrepreneur, is India's richest self-made woman billionaire, who is also the first woman to sign 'The Giving Pledge.' In September 2018, Biocon's market cap was Rs 37,350 crore. Today, Biocon is among the world's most respected producers of biologic drugs—which are complex large molecules produced by living organisms to fight diseases like cancer—and biosimilars— affordable biologic drugs which are not exact copies but are similar. Along with its partner Mylan, Biocon is also the first global company to get US Food and Drug Administration approval for two biosimilars to fight breast and stomach cancer as well as the side effects from chemotherapy.

---

* Interview conducted on 21 December 2018 when Kiran Mazumdar-Shaw was in Bengaluru

When the young Kiran Mazumdar graduated first in her class from university in Bangalore, her plans were completely different from what the future had in store for her. She wanted to be a doctor and was devastated when she didn't get into medical school. She then approached her father to ask him for 'capitation fees' of Rs 10,000, which would ensure a seat at a private medical college. He refused and told her something that she remembers even today. 'Money is not a currency to buy favours, money is a currency to make a difference,' he had said.

With that life lesson to guide her, she set off for a course in brewing in Australia to learn how to develop enzyme technologies to make beer. Her father was a master brewer at United Breweries, Bangalore. Little did she know then that destiny would lead her from beer technologies to anticancer drugs that are now prescribed by doctors around the world.

'I often joke by saying, India's largest biotech company was started because of gender bias—which is true, actually.' She laughs. 'In 1976, I had come back from Australia as India's first qualified female brewmaster, but I found it very difficult to get accepted as a woman in the field of brewing. No one would hire me. It was an accidental encounter with an Irish entrepreneur who had started a biotech company in Ireland that got me interested in starting a company in India. I didn't think about the enormous challenge that would come my way in starting India's first biotech company because I was so excited. I could apply the knowledge I had acquired from brewing to something similar like developing enzyme technologies. It was also my rebellious streak that made me take up the challenge. I was rejected by the brewing industry and I felt I had to show them I could run a business.'

However, in 1978, a year after the Emergency, a new government was in power and it was a time when the focus was on a much more protectionist economy and big businesses. 'Given that you had absolutely no business experience in a field which was so different, how did you manage?' I ask.

'I started Biocon in November 1978, when India was at the height of the Licence Raj. It was a time when there were fierce controls on foreign exchange, travel was highly regulated, and we couldn't carry more than $500 on a trip abroad. I was trying to embark on a technology-related start-up, so you can imagine how difficult it was.

'I realized I needed an import permit and licence, a tough thing to acquire. But the good thing was that I was also an export-oriented company, which made it a little easier for me to get an import licence.

'In hindsight,' she reminisces, 'it helped me to grow as a young woman, an entrepreneur, trying to start a new business in a sector that very few people understood. I had huge credibility challenges— the first year I struggled to even get debt financing, I had issues employing, hiring people, because they felt there was no job security. So, I was considered high risk on all fronts—a financial risk by the banks, an employment risk by potential employees. I also had other challenges which were really about how do I run my business with very frugal infrastructure.

'I needed basic instrumentation and reagents to work on research and development and enzyme manufacturing. However, despite all this, the journey was a learning process. I received help from the "babus" of the Licence Raj who, I think, felt sorry for me. They felt I needed help.'

According to Kiran Mazumdar-Shaw, then came India's big defining moment. The 1991 economic reforms ushered in by then prime minister Narasimha Rao and then finance minister Manmohan Singh transformed India's economic path decisively; it changed the lives of thousands of entrepreneurs and the larger Indian economy. The reforms had been spurred by a series of economic setbacks, including a balance-of-payments crisis where India's huge import bills had spiralled along with an increasing fiscal deficit, at one point leaving the country with only three weeks of foreign exchange reserves and a mortgage of nearly 47 tons of India's gold by the Chandra Shekhar government to avoid defaulting on international payments. The new Congress government took over in June 1991 and on 24 July 1991, Manmohan Singh read out his historic budget, abolishing import restrictions virtually overnight, opening up the banking and industrial sector and ushering in many other reforms.

'In 1991, when the economic reforms happened, that was *the* big turning point in the way we do things,' she recalls. 'For ten years, I had to struggle and fight for licences, even just building my company was a huge problem. I was battling for cement and steel allocation. The Asian Games were being held at the same time and all the available cement and steel was directed towards that project. I couldn't get it because it was rationed. We would get 10 tons of steel and 100 bags of cement given to us as ration every two to three weeks. A project that should've been completed in a year's time took three years.'

'When I heard Manmohan Singh's budget speech, it was music to my ears. It was historic and transformational for the Indian economy. It freed red tape, lifted controls from foreign exchange, lifted licences on many things, increased the ease of doing business and travelling—I remember all of it vividly. All that we are hearing today from the current government of the ease of doing business actually happened in 1991, from our perspective. The whole concept of ease of doing business was introduced in 1991 and it made a big impact on us.'

'India was at a precarious stage,' she says. 'As an entrepreneur operating outside India, India seemed to be on the brink of economic collapse because we did not even have enough gold. I mean, we had to almost trade gold to keep us afloat. That was a very scary thought.

However, when the reforms went through and things started easing up, I could visibly see that investing in technology, importing high-end equipment became so much easier. I started speeding up the pace of my research and product development. I found other companies trying to upgrade their technologies. So, there was a sort of multiplier effect.'

Kiran Mazumdar-Shaw took full advantage of the reforms to scale up her company, and she was thinking big. Unilever had a minority stake in her company, and she bought it back, with her husband John Shaw selling their property in London to fund her.

'How were you so convinced that you didn't need the support of one the world's corporate behemoths?' I ask.

'Our enzyme technology and the approach to "greening" businesses was an idea ahead of its time,' she replies confidently. 'Climate change and environmental sustainability weren't being discussed in the 1970s and '80s. In fact, it was one of the most polluting eras because post-reform India started investing heavily in manufacturing. Whether it was textiles, starch processing, pulp, industries flourished. But all of these were using highly polluting chemical technology. India's pharmaceutical industry boomed after that. We tried to introduce our eco-friendly enzyme technology as an alternative chemical technology, but nobody was interested because they thought it was more expensive in terms of upfront investment. Since there was no strict regulation, industries weren't particular in making investments in high-end effluent-treatment plants. So it was a tough time but like most entrepreneurs, we were very committed and focused on what we were trying to do. We didn't hesitate, we just got on with it.'

Biocon's first few years were all about survival, while the next ten years were about scaling up.

'In 1998, I began to ask myself a few hard questions. Was I in the right business? Were enzymes the right spot for me? Did it have potential for future growth?' she says. 'That was a defining moment for me because I realized that, perhaps, I would like to go beyond enzymes, into an area that could give me much higher growth. It is interesting that over a twenty-year-journey, my revenues were only 10 million dollars and my workforce was about five hundred people. Five years after our foray into biopharmaceuticals, my revenues increased tenfold to 100 million dollars and my workforce tripled,' she recounts, ever businesslike, about a time when she was also featured in *Time* magazine, *Forbes* and *Fortune* among the most influential people in Indian business.[†]

'The big breakthroughs, of course, were statins [one of the world's most widely used medicines, which helps lower "bad cholesterol" or low-density lipoprotein (LDL) and triglycerides], insulin and getting US FDA approval,' I say.

'When we decided to transfer the business from enzymes to biopharma, the two low-hanging fruits, the obvious opportunities, were insulins, statins and immunosuppressants. When it came to insulin, we had very interesting technology with which we developed some enzymes and the result was we had engineered a proprietary yeast technology. Even today, Biocon is the only company in the world to use this technology.

'We had a very good platform technology for developing enzymes using fungal fermentation. And I realized that it could help us develop statins. It worked. Today, it's very interesting that we are the "Intel inside" for 40 per cent of the world's statins and immunosuppressants and now making generic tablets [which share the same active ingredient as "branded medicine" or medicines made by the big pharma companies and provide the same health benefits but are much more affordable] too,' she concludes.

---

† http://content.time.com/time/specials/packages/
article/0,28804,1984685_1984949_1985233,00.html; https://www.
forbes.com/lists/2008/11/biz_powerwomen08_Kiran-Mazumdar-Shaw_
OW2K.html; https://www.fortuneindia.com/mpw/kiran-mazumdar-
shaw?year=2018

In the 1980s, the Indian technology and IT revolution was sparked in Bangalore. It was a new economy virtually headquartered in the city. Kiran Mazumdar-Shaw watched this unfold around her.

'During the 1980s, IT businesses began to take shape. I knew the Infosys team really well; we were almost next-door neighbours. I watched companies like Infosys, Wipro and others take off and grow. Many traditional industries were left scratching their heads. I still remember meeting the head of British American Tobacco, who told me that they just didn't know how to deal with what was happening in the world because the IT companies were flummoxing them with the kind of values and multiples they were commanding, in terms of arriving at their market cap. Even if they had real and large businesses, their market caps weren't as great as the new IT companies. It's plain crazy.'

A crazy but exhilarating time, during which Bangalore had become the world's outsourcing capital for tech services, so much so that the phrase 'being Bangalored' became popular when describing jobs in the US moving to India's new Silicon Valley.

The IT climate was ripe and so, in 1994, Kiran Mazumdar-Shaw also set up a research services company called Syngene.

'The reasoning was that if IT companies could offer their services for financial solutions, I too could offer research services to pharma and biotech companies. Things were happening in Bangalore in a very different way. We were all focusing on technology in the new exciting, evolving world of IT, digital and biotech. We were relatively unaffected by any kind of government regulations because we were comparatively unregulated up to the 1990s. Even today, I think Bangalore is quite far removed from what is happening in the rest of the country. We are almost like an island of technology excellence.'

'And then something truly exciting happened. The government in Karnataka, which has always been pragmatic and forward-looking, reached out to private-sector tech companies for help with policy scripting. This was a bold experiment for any state government at that time. Even today, Karnataka is the only state where policy think tanks and vision groups are headed by private-sector people like me, Mohandas Pai, Kris Gopalakrishnan and so on. Nowhere else do they ever experiment with such things,' she says.

'We were the first state that came up with an IT policy and a biotech policy, and that tradition continues,' Kiran Mazumdar-Shaw says. 'Karnataka is the first state now to come up with government policies and plans for electric vehicles, we are the first ones that came up with a start-up policy, a rare-disease policy and we are coming up with a drone policy now.'

What is also a first about the Bangalore tech economy is that it was started by first-generation entrepreneurs with very little capital but also with little dependence on government, unlike traditional businesses which needed government help on issues like land and industrial licences.

'We all started with the same model of debt financing,' Kiran says proudly. 'All of us have funded our businesses in a smart and intelligent way, so there was no question of crony capitalism or politicians doing us favours. The moment our businesses became profitable, we were all relatively debt-free, because we kept ploughing back profits into the business to grow it further. In fact, most Bangalore start-ups began at a time when India had a very socialistic command and control economy, where businesses had to comply with hundreds of government regulations. So then big businesses found ways to bend the rules. That was how the "Licence Raj" came to be. That was a big mistake. India created large-sized public-sector undertakings, which today, unfortunately, are mostly almost defunct. The government felt that the private sector didn't have enough capital or financial lustre to do things on their own. Therefore, the government would tell entrepreneurs—"Here's a licence and here is some money and every time you need more keep coming back to us, but we will decide how your product is going to be sold and procured and we will decide how much to tax you." But that's why tech businesses were different. We were not dependent on domestic consumption at all. The tech business was all about exports, so we didn't need any government favours, and we were happy that we were out of their clutches.'

It's no wonder, then, that Bangalore's entrepreneurs ensure they stay very far from Delhi's corridors of power; from Infosys to Wipro and the new breed of start-ups, they are all headquartered in the city. However, what differentiates Kiran Mazumdar-Shaw from other Delhi and Mumbai business leaders is her willingness to speak out about national issues, both online and offline.

'Apart from being a business leader, I am also a citizen of this country,' she says. 'I care about this country's economic future and therefore, I tweet about issues, whether it's education, healthcare or policy, that are important. And that is also why a few Bangalorean colleagues and I started the Bangalore Political Action Committee. The idea behind it is to try and build good governance in our political system. We want a cadre of political leaders who are focused on good governance.

'What I appreciate about the Modi government is that they have focused on good governance and anti-corruption measures. But whether they been objective about it is a point of debate! However, I do subscribe to the philosophy that India can only be a great nation if we have integrity, honesty and zero corruption.'

Kiran Mazumdar-Shaw is both a business and thought leader. However, why is it that a self-made woman billionaire like her is still a rarity in twenty-first century India?

'Forty years later, you are still often the only woman in the room. Why haven't business leaders like yourself been able to pass this forward?' I ask.

'When I was building my company, for the first twenty years, my leadership team comprised 60 per cent women. We were only 100 people. To have so many women on the board was quite something in the 1980s. When we got into biopharma, we needed to scale up tenfold. We needed to bring in new capabilities and new skills, and unfortunately, we couldn't find too many women. Suddenly, the gender ratio became skewed and was flipped—60 per cent men and 40 per cent women. It still concerns and worries me that at the leadership level today, we have only 30 per cent women, which is very low especially since that I am the head of the company and I am a woman. I haven't been able to grow more women leaders. So today I make a conscious effort to groom women in middle management and help them move up to leadership roles. Mostly, it is about credibility building. Most women are unable to earn the credibility that men earn very easily.'

'How does a woman entrepreneur build credibility?' I ask.

'Be very focused on what you are doing and deliver. That's how you earn credibility. I learnt that the hard way. When I was focused on biosimilars, I was criticized. There were people who said that I didn't know what I was doing, that I was playing with shareholder money, that I was wasting too much money in R&D, that as a woman, I should learn from the men. Today, however, the same gossipmongers praise me on online platforms, saying how the men should learn from me.' She smiles wryly.

'You described the defining moment for India's economy as the 1991 reforms. Twenty-eight years later, do you feel we need another 1991 moment?' I ask.

'I feel we have missed a golden opportunity,' she says. 'Everyone thought that the Modi government would step up the reforms in a big way but what we saw was below expectations. I am personally disappointed that a lot of what was talked about in campaign speeches in 2014 was not converted into real, pragmatic policies. We now need jobs for a new economy that is moving away from the brick-and-mortar format. We should not be looking at creating only manufacturing jobs to replace the jobs lost in agriculture. Today, the reason behind agrarian distress is because the sharing of value is not equitable in the agriculture value chain. For example, take the case of a rice farmer and the end product. A rice packet costs Rs 100. What is the farmer's share? You will find that it is only Re 1. Therefore, one must ensure that there is equitable distribution of value in the agricultural chain.

'Also, the transition to alternative jobs is driven by the need for better earnings and this is dependent on the availability of opportunities. Today, if a farmer or farm labourer can become an Ola driver, that's a very good jump in livelihood, because as a farmer he would be earning subsistence farming rates while as an Ola driver his earning power increases substantially. There is so much potential with regards to jobs of the future and the new economy.

'Just look at easy things like robotics—we should be using this to tackle manual scavenging, or the removal of human waste and the cleaning of sewers, which is done by labourers currently. Think about the number of jobs it will create, because someone has to make the robots, someone has to develop the software, someone has to operate the robots, right? It does a better job and minimizes danger and the horrible aspect of lack of dignity that is associated with manual scavenging.'

These are simple and effective ideas and perhaps that's why Delhi needs to listen to voices from across the country on the next big economic reform.

Meanwhile, Kiran Mazumdar-Shaw has a larger vision for social change. For her, the fight against cancer will be the next frontier and a personal one as well.

'A blockbuster drug is not, as people call it, a billion-dollar drug. It is about serving a billion patients. That to me is a true blockbuster drug. Cancer, "the Emperor of all Maladies" as Siddhartha Mukherjee calls it, has always been very challenging. I've seen cancer up close. My best friend died of cancer, my mother had a bout of cancer, my husband has gone through cancer, and I know how tough and expensive it is to treat and deal with this disease. I wanted to provide affordable access to life-saving new cancer drugs and that is why

I am very proud of the drugs we have developed, especially to treat breast cancer, which has helped thousands of women in India. It used to cost almost tenfold more than what it does today thanks to our drugs. Now, we are looking at new technologies that can actually cure many difficult cancers. I believe that in the years ahead, cancer will be like any other chronic disease—a very managed one.'

And when Kiran Mazumdar-Shaw believes in something, she makes it happen. She may regret she didn't get into medical school but her contribution to the world of medical science has literally been a lifesaver.

[14]

Sania Mirza

Match Point

Sania Mirza lives life on her own terms, which is not surprising for someone who has charted her own path since the age of twelve, going where no Indian sportswoman has gone before in terms of world rankings and sporting achievements. She didn't set out to be a role model but the Sania Effect—as it came to be known—led to thousands of little girls picking up a tennis racket for the first time. After Sania came a series of women athletes—Saina Nehwal, P.V. Sindhu, Dipa Karmakar, Mary Kom, Mithali Raj and others who are household names today. But Sania paved the way. At thirty-two, she's on a temporary hiatus to be a full-time mom, but she's already preparing to be back where she's truly home—on a tennis court.*

---

* Interview conducted in January 2019 when Sania Mirza was in Hyderabad

When Sania first began playing tennis at the age of six, under the watchful eye of her father in Hyderabad, she had never dreamt an Indian could be number one. In those days, tennis was unheard of in the relatively sleepy city of the Charminar.

'We used to play on courts made of cow dung,' she says.

'Courts made of cow dung? That's a first!' I say.

'Yes,' she says, laughing. 'We literally used to play on courts made of crap. There were no clay courts, no hard courts. We'd play on whatever surface we got, getting tetanus injections before playing, in case we fell. People used to make fun of us—my family and me—saying: "Do you think she's going to become Martina Hingis?" At that time Martina Hingis was at top of the game and ironically, I was able to achieve so much later with Martina at my side.'

'When did you believe you had it in you to be the first Indian woman to make it to the top of international tennis rankings?' I ask.

'My goals were always extremely immediate, things I thought I could achieve,' Sania says matter-of-factly. 'Between the ages of six and eight, I never said I wanted to be world number one. I would say that one day I wanted to play at Wimbledon because, at that point in time, it seemed achievable, even as a dream. As I became better, my goals kept changing. I never believed in comfort zones even when I was a very young girl. I was always doing what hadn't been done by anyone before. That was just the way I was and if someone told me I couldn't do something, I would definitely try to do it. That was the little hidden rebel in me, I guess.'

However, the big mental breakthrough came early enough, when Sania was just twelve years old and won the under-14 and the under-16 nationals, on the same day.

'That was the day when Adidas sponsored me. I was twelve years old and that day, I truly felt that I was meant for bigger things. I'm meant to dream bigger than playing at Wimbledon, I'm meant to dream that I can win Wimbledon, I'm meant to dream of being world number one. This happened six years after I had begun playing tennis, and it was the moment when I knew I wanted tennis to be my life,' she recounts emphatically.

The first major validation of that decision came in 2003, when Sania went to Junior Wimbledon, and surprised India and the international tennis world. Her world changed overnight, and dramatically.

'As an Indian sportsperson, as someone who represents a young, new generation of Indian women athletes, what were the defining moments in your life, which, in turn, have also defined Indian sport?' I ask.

'I think I've been very fortunate to have many defining moments for myself, personally,' says Sania. 'But being the first woman to do so many things as a tennis player, for instance, winning Junior Wimbledon [Sania won the girls' doubles in 2003 along with Russian player Alisa Kleybanova] was also extremely defining for tennis in India. As a country, we started taking notice when I was sixteen and won at Wimbledon. We then had a tennis player and a girl who played at the top level and was able to compete with the best.

'I was a very shy girl,' she reminisces. 'When I was young, I was one of those girls who knew the answer but wouldn't raise their hand in class. I never liked the attention, I didn't like all eyes on me and ironically, I've had to do that every day of my life after that, since I was sixteen. I had also become used to being the only girl at this level—there were a couple of boys, but then they started dropping off. I became sure that this was it, I was going to move forward and it's going to be me alone. Then the Junior Wimbledon [doubles] happened and suddenly there was a huge increase in media attention and everyone knew my name. I was just fifteen going on sixteen.

When I came back to India, suddenly there were people waiting for me in the airport. I felt as though it was the biggest thing that was ever going to happen to me because that was also my first taste of stardom. It was even sweeter because it was a hard-fought win. We had played on court number two in the finals and we lost the first set. We had also been the last people to enter the draw and then we won the next one. Then we went through and it was probably the most special I've ever felt winning a tournament. Even when compared to the things I achieved later, this win may rank lower, but it is still one of my most important achievements.'

From Junior Wimbledon in 2003 to the big Grand Slam wins in 2009 and the Wimbledon doubles win with Martina Hingis in 2015, on the road to number-one rankings in the world, Sania charted a series of firsts for any Indian in tennis.

Along with the highs, however, Sania has had her lows, including injuries and a severe bout with depression. There have been many tough moments in her career, she admits.

'I played singles virtually my whole life, until 2012. But I had to make a tough choice. It was taking a toll on my body. I had a form of arthritis, so the choice was either to reset my goals and try to get to number one in doubles and win Grand Slams or remain at about eighty or ninety ranking in singles because that's what my body was allowing me to do. There was a time when I went into depression for a few months because I had to retire from a wrist injury at the Beijing Olympics in 2008. I was so depressed that I didn't even leave my room, I was barely eating. It was very severe. I had to snap out of it if I wanted to play tennis again. For one, I've had three surgeries [for her knees and her right wrist] and each one is both physically, mentally and emotionally taxing. You ask yourself if you can trust your body, you question if you're going to be able to play at the same level again. It's a very emotionally draining and a tough situation to come out of.

'That's when my family came into play. They made me stand up and make me believe I could do it again.'

Once Sania reset her goals, she found her career progressing rapidly. With different partners, she proved to be a natural at doubles.

'My first Grand Slam win was in 2009 at the Australian Open with Mahesh Bhupathi, in mixed doubles,' says Sania. 'And I think that was very special because he was my best friend and a fellow Indian. It was also my first-ever Grand Slam.

'My favourite one, however, was my Wimbledon win with Martina in 2015. We were in the third set and we were about to lose. We began in bright daylight and finished under the floodlights, like a movie setting. We had goosebumps when we came out from the dramatic finale at centre court with the score 5–7, 7–6, 7–5. It was incredible, and winning that at that time, the way we did, was a really special experience.'

It was an adrenaline-filled final with Hingis–Mirza coming back after being down in the third set and the game being the first women's doubles Grand Slam win for Sania. 'The fact that you were now partnering with the same Martina, whom you were told as a young girl you could never become, must have made it extra special,' I say.

'We had played each other quite a bit,' she says. 'And I think I won a couple of times and she won a couple of times. She's a legend, and to win against her is very special. Also, as you said, so many memories came to my mind at the time, like the things people used to say, but I've never done anything to prove a point to someone or else I wouldn't be playing tennis. The victory against her and with her was for myself.

'Another victory was definitely becoming number one in the world [in women's doubles] on 12 April 2015. It was my anniversary too, so I remember it very clearly,' she says with a laugh. 'So, yes, as a nation, as a person, it's a dream to become number one at anything you do in the world, let alone at a global sport like tennis. That, I feel, brought a sense of belief. So, when I met young girls after that, they perhaps believed that they too could be the best. I feel that we mostly don't really think of ourselves like that, because India is not a country where tennis is considered a mass sport. Everyone plays cricket, now football, but tennis is not something we believe we can be champions at. I would imagine the feat I achieved and having stayed there for two years would be very defining for the country in sports.'

That is why one of Sania's most important achievements has been an intangible one—being the first of a galaxy of Indian women champions in the world of sport, a true role model to future generations. When she started out, she was virtually the lone flag bearer.

She agrees. 'The only woman athlete I had heard of before was P.T. Usha and that was because she was so phenomenal. She was the only one wannabe women athletes could look up to. I think, at the time, P.T. Usha was competing full force, however, the media and TV weren't as all-pervading, so it was difficult to create such an impact. So, in a way, being the first Indian woman athlete to make an international breakthrough was great—it comes with a lot of praise and admiration—but it's also the toughest to be the first at anything because there's no path to follow. There is no one to look up to, you have to dream for yourself, and you have to believe in yourself. It's a lot easier to say, oh, Sachin Tendulkar has done it, so I will also be able to do it, but there was no one for me. I had to find my heroes outside of my sport or find heroes from outside India. Steffi Graf was my idol while growing up and she still is in many ways. That's what really changed after everything I achieved, by the grace of God, because girls today can say, I want to become like Sania or I want to be better than her. I always tell them to be better than me, because at least there is a sort of benchmark they want to reach, which makes a big difference.'

She notes that the number of Indian women sportspersons making their mark today is very impressive, especially given the Indian mindset, where girls are supposed to be pretty and cook and not become dark by playing in the sun.

'Sport is also frowned upon,' Sania says, 'because it involves girls going out and playing in shorts or skirts.'

And that is why it's laudable that even with such entrenched thinking there are so many women champions one can name today. Ten years ago, Sania didn't believe that any of this could have been achieved. Outside of cricket, the biggest sport stars in the country are women today. 'That's progress right there,' she says proudly.

Yet, I point out, that despite the standout performance by women sportspersons, they often drop out when faced with the politics of sports, whether it is indifferent coaches, biased selectors, lack of facilities, or even just an undermining remark. Whether it's a Mithali Raj or Jwala Gutta or even Sania Mirza, all of them have faced flak from sports administrators. For the 2012 London Olympics, the tennis association had insisted Sania partner with Leander Paes in the mixed doubles rather than her regular partner Mahesh Bhupathi. It was a trade-off for Leander agreeing to play in the Olympics men's doubles with a junior teammate. Sania went public with her unhappiness. In a statement then she said, 'As an Indian woman belonging to the twenty-first century, what I find disillusioning is the humiliating manner in which I was put up as bait to try and pacify one of the disgruntled stalwarts of Indian tennis.'

'I mean, why was I being told to do anything, at the end of the day? I had just won a Grand Slam. It was plain and simple sexism,' she says, recalling the incident.

Beyond sport, Sania's outspokenness also made her a potent symbol of women empowerment, which can be daunting for a sixteen-year-old facing the public eye.

'I was always myself,' she replies. 'That *was* my biggest strength and it *is* my biggest strength. Being scared that you're going to be judged because of what you do or say or eat or drink is not something that I have learnt to do. My parents instilled these values in me and my sister, that as long as we're not wronging anyone and we believe what we're doing is correct, we should do it, and say it. I've always said what's in my heart. Really, I'm all heart and not brain at all. In the process I became this girl or woman, and then people were like, wow, she's empowering! As a representative for the United Nations [Sania became the first South Asian woman to become a UN Women goodwill ambassador], I always maintain that empowerment has to come from within, not the outside. You have to believe you're equal and you're empowered for people to give you that respect.

'In fact,' she points out indignantly, 'after everything I've achieved, people still ask me if I have a brother and when I tell them that I don't, it's like a tragedy. They believe that having a boy in the family would have changed something. Our colonial mindset goes very deep in our culture in Asia. We have to fight against that mindset and change it. It won't change in one generation, it'll take a few generations.'

Sania has had more than her fair share of pressure, both on and off the court. From clerics criticizing the length of her skirts to tennis politics and her marriage to former Pakistan captain and cricketer, Shoaib Malik, she has fought to live life her way. Her steel comes through as we talk about this.

'One of the toughest things to do is to grow up in front of the media. You're so young and you don't even know who you are. You're chubby, you have pimples on your face, you're still finding the person that you are, and I had to do that in public. And that's the reason I'm a bit weird,' she says with a laugh. 'It's not easy to be questioned about things at sixteen when all you care about is bunking school or college and going for a movie. Back then, I was answering questions about certain things that had nothing to do with my tennis either.'

'You married a popular cricketer from Pakistan. Did it hurt when you were called Pakistan's daughter-in-law? Did you ever have second thoughts about marrying a person from Pakistan, given the tense relations between both countries and the flak you knew you would face? Did you ever feel targeted because of your religious identity or your choices?' I ask.

'No, I did not,' she responds immediately. 'That's not the mindset me or my husband grew up with. We were never taught to look at the country, colour or religion people came from. I believe your intuition with someone is person to person; it's not about where they're from or the political scenario between their countries. That's my attitude towards everybody, whether it is my friends, my family or my husband. The thing is, being a celebrity and from a very young age in my life, I became very thick-skinned and that's also helped. Especially with social media today, everyone has this unknown voice, sitting behind screens and saying whatever they want, being extremely daring because they're anonymous while celebrities have become a very soft target. So, whether I married someone from Pakistan or not, there are many celebrities who aren't married to someone from Pakistan but are still targeted. It's always something or the other, and as celebrities, we have to get accustomed to the fact that people will always have their opinions. At the end of the day, I always say, we have a country of 1 billion people, if 2 million people don't like you, it still doesn't mean anything.'

'Shoaib Malik cheers for India when you play tennis and you cheer for Pakistan when he's playing a match. That's a great example of a successful marriage, of two well-known sportspeople in their own right,' I say.

She nods. 'I go and watch his matches, and I support his team and want them to win, but most importantly, I want him to play well and he does the same, and we always joke about it. It's really not that dramatic as people want it to be. Oh, if his team will play India what will happen? It's just another cricket match and it's just another tennis match and that's what sport has taught us. Humanity is above everything else.

'Being married to a fellow sportsperson has its advantages and its challenges, like every marriage,' Sania continues. 'There are many things that are understood, which don't have to be explained. Like when you lose a match, you don't have to explain why you are in a bad mood. He won't say let's go out for a dinner or party. We both understand the mindset we're in before a big game or after a big game, win or lose. We both understand the pressures we feel playing for our respective countries. However, it obviously comes with other challenges, like we are apart a lot, we're in high-pressure jobs, so sometimes we take it out on the other. So, in some ways, it's like every other marriage. However, to be married to a very strong woman you have to be a very strong man. It takes a secure man, a man who has a very wide range of ideas, who can adapt, and he has all those qualities, which is why we've been able to have a successful nine-year marriage.'

Successful, and a marriage of equal partnership. Both Sania and Shoaib travel the world for their sport, spend time in their homes in India and Pakistan, and share a home in Dubai. Even more delightfully, Sania and Shoaib's first child, Izhaan, shares their last names, Mirza-Malik. She credits this decision to both of them.

'We believe in equality and that the child should know not just his paternal roots but also his maternal roots,' she says proudly.

Interestingly, motherhood has changed the ever-competitive Sania. Even though the Olympics are coming soon, for once, Sania isn't setting herself medal goals. She's taking it slow as she plans her return. While Serena and other well-known tennis moms are showing that babies and competitive sport can go together, Sania is also discovering a new side to herself.

'To be very honest, it's given me a feeling of selflessness, which I didn't think I had,' she says. 'Athletes are a bit selfish as people. Our whole job and life revolve around winning and it's all about us—what I want to do, when I want to eat, when I want to train, when I want to sleep, when I want to wake up. So, when I became pregnant and felt the baby moving, I wanted everything in the world for the baby even more than I wanted it for myself. After the baby has come into my life, that feeling has just multiplied. If it means giving up what I want for myself, then I will. So, I'd say motherhood has helped me evolve into a better person,' she says, smiling contentedly.

Mellowed and happy in her space, with nothing left to prove to the world or herself, Sania's defining contribution to Indian sport has been her ability to give young girls the belief to dream, and dream big, of becoming world champions—on their own terms.

[15]

Sachin Tendulkar

On the Field of Dreams

Sachin Tendulkar is one of the greatest cricketers the world has ever seen. When he retired in 2013, Sachin held the record for the highest number of centuries in test cricket, the highest run-scorer, the highest number of 'Man of the Match' awards. And in one-day cricket, the highest number of centuries, highest numbers of fifties, to name a few. However, his contribution to India was indefinably greater than just statistics or sporting achievements. With cricket being such an important part of India's national fabric, Sachin symbolized a dedication and commitment to an ideal in which the individual batted for the larger good. Perhaps, that's why it's only fitting he became the first sportsperson, and the youngest too, to receive India's highest honour, the Bharat Ratna.*

* Interview conducted on 5 October 2018, Mumbai

As we sit in Sachin Tendulkar's home office surrounded by trophies of his landmark innings, the man known as the 'God of Indian cricket', even in his retirement, comes alive when he talks about his cricket journey. When the diminutive genius walked out on the pitch, so did a billion Indians. Yet his shoulders proved, time and again, broad enough for a billion aspirations. When he faltered, we blamed him, when he won—and what victories they were—it was our collective victory.

The longest journeys begin with the smallest steps. And for Sachin, he didn't play cricket to emulate a star batsman or cricketer, he didn't want to be a Bradman or Gavaskar as a little boy.

'The reason I started playing cricket was my brother, Ajit,' he says. 'I wanted to be like him. I was just ten years old and we would play cricket in our colony in front of the building. We'd spend the whole afternoon in our summer holidays playing in the scorching heat—nothing would bother me.'

'From emulating your elder brother to cricket becoming an abiding passion for you till today, what transformed the game for you?' I ask.

'The first defining moment in my life—when I seriously thought about becoming a cricketer—was in 1983 when we [India] won the World Cup. I didn't know much about cricket at the time,' he says. 'To be honest, I didn't even know that after 6 balls are bowled the field, not the batsmen, changes. In our building, the batsmen would change because of the limited space available. I only learnt that later on. All I knew then was that it gave me a lot of happiness,' he says, smiling.

'In fact, when we won the World Cup, I didn't know the significance of winning it either,' he says.

In 1983, India entered the World Cup cricket finals for the first time and were playing against arguably the best team in the world at the time—the West Indies. Led by captain Kapil Dev, their win was celebrated across the country.

'I still remember, in the evening, my friends went to the neighbourhood park and celebrated, and I didn't understand why it was so big; I was celebrating because *they* were celebrating. But you know that sight of Kapil Dev holding the World Cup—it is still so fresh in my mind. That was one moment where I said, "I want to do this one day. I want to hold that trophy,"' muses Sachin.

When Kapil's devils, as they were called, went from underdogs to beating the mighty West Indians, it gave the entire nation a sense that we could win the big battles. This was history being made, a victory that went beyond sports.

'The 1983 World Cup victory transformed our belief about ourselves as a cricketing nation. How did it change you as a ten-year-old?' I ask.

'It had a huge impact on me,' he says. 'From then on, things started changing gradually. I spent time at Shivaji Park with Achrekar sir [Ramakant Achrekar was Sachin's first coach]. I spent my entire summer holidays with him. That's when Achrekar sir approached my father and asked if it would be okay to change my school. I moved from the New English School in Bandra to Shardashram because they had a better cricket team. They invariably reached the finals and won a number of school tournaments. So, I started playing there, did well, and then came my debut.'

And what a debut it was! The Sachin story had already begun spreading across Mumbai when memorably, as a teenager, he faced his idol Kapil Dev's bowling at the nets. Selected to play for Mumbai at just fourteen, Sachin went on to score centuries in his first appearances at the Ranji and Duleep trophies. It was increasingly clear that his talent, and bat, could not be ignored. Then came his first international tour in November 1989 to Karachi, Pakistan. It was the tour that transformed Sachin Tendulkar, a boy wonder, into a cricketer.

At sixteen years old, Sachin was India's youngest cricketer ever to be selected in a test team, part of the eleven-member Indian squad all set to face some of the world's best fast bowlers from Imran Khan to Waqar Younis. As if that wasn't daunting enough, playing Pakistan on their home ground was a whole different ball game as the young Sachin was soon to find out.

Sachin smiles as he recalls that series. 'My debut series with Pakistan was without a doubt a defining moment in my career. At sixteen years, I didn't understand this rivalry and to what extent players pushed themselves especially when it was an India–Pakistan match. It was an acid test for me to go from domestic cricket to international cricket—that is in itself a big jump—but then I went to Pakistan and played the best bowling attack in the world. After my first outing [Sachin was bowled out for 15 in the first test by Waqar Younis, who was also making his debut], I remember walking back to the dressing room embarrassed, disappointed, and in tears. I went to the bathroom and I looked at myself and thought—"This is your first and last test match. You're not good enough to play for India."'

Luckily for India, Sachin's older teammates rallied around him.

'That's when my teammates calmed me down. They taught me real-life lessons—that I could only learn from my mistakes, that it was important to spend some time in the middle, that this was not a school match, I was playing against the best, and that I should respect the fact that I would not be able to hit every ball; if I felt that the pace was too much, well, everyone felt that way. I had to give myself time. On that tour there were two moments where I felt I was heading down south and I'd lost hope. Then, in the next test match I scored 59 runs and it restored my confidence,' he remembers.

'The crunch moment in that series came in the fourth test match. India was batting in the second innings with a day and a half to go,' Sachin continues. 'Till then, we had drawn three test matches.

So, we were doing really well, and Pakistan was desperate to win the series; they had a better fast-bowling attack. They had Imran, Wasim, Waqar and the fourth fast bowler kept changing in every test match. We were 34–4 when I got hit on my nose with a fast ball from Waqar. I broke my nose, but I continued batting, and we saved that test match.'

He recounts the story matter-of-factly today, but as a young boy of sixteen facing a Pakistani fast-bowling attack and then continuing to bat with a broken nose after refusing medical help must have been excruciatingly painful. Then captain Imran Khan had apparently told his bowlers—all much older than the teenager—to specifically target Sachin.

'What kept you going?' I question.

'Well,' he says, 'I had heard many stories where batsmen had been hit. It either makes or breaks them. Fortunately, in my case, I became fearless. My brother was also there watching the game and I remember at tea time, I was batting on some 8 or 10 runs and while going up, my brother just looked at me and I said, "I'm okay, don't worry."'

He was better than okay. The Pakistan tour was a trial by fire which the teenager passed with flying colours. I wonder if Imran Khan (now the Prime Minister of Pakistan), and others in the Pakistan team, realized at the time that they had blooded a future cricketing legend. 'Did they ever apologize for the way they targeted you?' I ask.

'We never discussed it,' he says with a smile. 'Yes, there were moments when they could've been better but at the end, on the field, it's ruthless. Nothing else matters. The whole country is looking up to you with high expectations. If my heart tells me, yes, you've done your best, then that's all that matters.'

After that, milestones kept falling by the wayside. A series of tough tours—Pakistan, New Zealand and England—followed. In fact, out of Sachin's first twenty test matches, nineteen were played abroad. It was on the England tour that he scored his first century.

'Even though I made my debut in 1989, the first test match that I played in India was in 1993 against England. When I scored my first 100 in England, I'd like to believe that, at least in those days, I had cemented my place in the team. Slowly the team management started showing a lot of confidence in me. I got promoted to number four; I was number six or seven in the batting order. Then, in Australia, I started batting at number four. All these moments contributed to my cricket journey.'

As records continued to be broken, Sachin's cricketing stature grew. Importantly, his belief in Team India and putting the game first also stood out. Even as chants of 'Sachin! Sachin!' drowned out everything else when he walked on to the field, he never let it go to his head. Perhaps the moment that best defines Sachin Tendulkar's character is his father's death during the 1999 World Cup. Sachin, who was extremely close to his father, was devastated. He flew back to India for just one day and then came right back to play for India, scoring 140 runs against Kenya.

'Was that a difficult decision to take?' I ask.

Sachin, ever self-effacing, responds, 'It wasn't my decision. It was my family's decision. You must have people who advise you to do the right thing. All my family members, my mother, my wife felt that I should go back and that is what my father would have wanted, so I did that, even though it was very difficult for me. On one TV interview, after that match, I had to wear my sunglasses. I've never done that before, but I couldn't control my tears every time I spoke about my father and I didn't want to cry in front of the cameras. Even when we were warming up, my eyes were constantly red. There were many times when I was playing that match and I kept looking up because I felt he was watching over me. It's difficult to express what I felt at the time. Every individual has to go through this, and we all have our own challenges that we have to overcome.'

From Sachin's individual challenges of performance and personal losses to the larger challenges of being an Indian cricketer . . . cricket in India is more than just a sport. It's almost sacrilege if India loses or a player fails. Whether it's the fans or the media scrutiny, the feedback can be brutal.

Sachin, too, wasn't immune to this. His tenure as captain was short-lived, leaving him, as he describes in his autobiography, *Playing It My Way*, 'scarred' and 'devastated'. The media used terms like 'Endulkar' to debate whether it was time for him to retire. Controversy began to dog Indian cricket's most-loved player. Yet, he stayed the course, letting his bat and his actions, on and off the field, do the talking.

'Cricket taught me patience and how to prepare for life,' he says. 'For me, what went on in the dressing room mattered the most because we knew what we had planned and how much we'd been able to execute that plan. Outsiders don't know what's happening in the dressing room. It's good to know what's happening in the outside world, but there comes a stage where you need to shut the doors and think about the game.'

'Were there any moments when you wanted to just quit? What were the toughest moments, Sachin?' I ask.

He doesn't mince his words, answering immediately. 'The 2007 World Cup.'

India had crashed out of the opening round of the 2007 World Cup in the West Indies, losing to teams like Bangladesh and Sri Lanka under coach Greg Chappell. The coach had decided to move Sachin down the batting order from number one to four. Sachin later wrote about how bad things were at the time, with the breakdown in relations with the coach who he referred to as a 'ringmaster who imposed his ideas on the players'. At one time, he'd even suggested to the Board of Control for Cricket in India (BCCI) that Greg Chappell should be left behind when India went for the World Cup as the open spat between Greg Chappell and senior players like Sachin, V.V.S. Laxman and Sourav Ganguly had lowered team morale.

'This was the moment when I came back home because I felt the right decisions in the team's interest were not being taken,' Sachin says. 'The thought process was different, and I was not particularly fond of that kind of planning. Also, we didn't qualify for the World Cup. Everything kept adding to the disappointment and there came a point when I told my brother that I didn't want to continue. I wasn't enjoying playing like this. My brother just told me one thing: "Imagine yourself holding that trophy in 2011."'

'You've mentioned life lessons learnt in the dressing room. What are the life lessons you've learnt from failures like these?' I ask.

'The importance of my family,' he answers. 'They taught me the values that I brought to the field. Nothing happens overnight; this generation wants everything right now. I say, you can have everything right *or* now, not both.'

From then on, however, things began to change. A new team management was brought in and Sachin soldiered on. From being out of the 2007 World Cup to the dramatic one in 2011, it was a whole different ball game.

The 2011 World Cup was Sachin's sixth. The final match against Sri Lanka was held in his home town, Mumbai. It had been twenty-eight years since India had won a world cup. But 2 April 2011 was India and Sachin's night.

The winning moment came with a 6 from M.S. Dhoni, and the country erupted in jubilation. From Sonia Gandhi in Delhi to Amitabh Bachchan in Mumbai, everybody spilt out on to the streets in spontaneous celebration, waving the national flag. Fittingly, Sachin was the highest run-scorer for India in the world cup.

'It kind of completed the journey. This was where I'd started and here I was, in my home town,' he says, smiling as he recalls that day. 'The way the entire country celebrated that night was incredible! Without a doubt, it was the best cricketing day of my life. I never thought it would take us so long to get from Wankhede Stadium to the Taj in Colaba. If I had started walking, I would have beat the bus we were in. It was all worth it because that moment was something which is never going to be repeated in my life,' he says.

India and the team recognized Sachin's contribution to the win. The team spontaneously carried him on their shoulders as they took a victory lap of the stadium. Interestingly, this was Sachin's final world cup and a young Virat Kohli's first. 'He's carried the burden of the nation for twenty-one years so it's time we carry him on our shoulders,' said Virat after the game.

'A journey that began at Lords in 1983 was completed at Wankhede Stadium in 2011. How do you think a country's psyche changes after a victory like that? How does it bring a nation together?' I ask.

'It's not just about cricket,' Sachin replies. 'It's any sport. While celebrating a win like this, people forget about their personal sorrows. We all have our challenges, but sport has the power to make you forget your personal problems and celebrate the occasion.'

Cricket has been larger than a game, it has been a unifying force. How does he see the future of Indian cricket now under Virat Kohli?

'The future of cricket is really bright,' says Sachin. 'We've got a combination of really good senior guys, a few guys who have played for nine to ten years which is a long enough period, and talented youngsters. So, it's a blend of three generations playing together. This is a positive sign for Indian cricket. I'm almost certain about that, but there are no guarantees in sports. The Indian team is much stronger than the other teams.'

Sachin's son, Arjun, is now part of a next generation of cricketers. He often talks about his family—his parents, brother, wife and children—being his key support system. Now that his daughter has just graduated and his son is beginning his cricket journey, Sachin finally has time to spend with them. 'You were constantly on tour during their growing-up years; what is it like reconnecting with them?'

'It was really tough for Arjun's first six years,' he says. 'He wouldn't talk to me, not even a word on the phone when I was travelling, so that became difficult for me. I would become worried. He was completely cut off from me. But when I got back, he would forget the rest of the world—that was his way of handling the situation. My daughter, Sara, was more understanding, it was easier to communicate with her.'

'Playing cricket isn't easy when you're Sachin Tendulkar's son. Are there huge expectations?' I ask.

'I never forced my son to play cricket,' Sachin replies. 'My daughter studies biomedical sciences. I don't think Anjali [Sachin's wife Anjali is a qualified doctor] has ever forced her into it. Our only condition was that they had to give their hundred per cent, whatever field they chose. Success is not guaranteed, but hard work is. I've told them, "I'm not going to judge you on your results, as long as you've done your best. I'll never put any pressure."'

'Finally, what do you think will be the Sachin legacy to Indian cricketers and the nation?'

'I was very proud about walking on to the field,' answers Sachin. 'I pushed myself as hard as I could and that included every practice session. I was happy with my game, but I was never satisfied. Having played with more than one generation of cricketers, it was a learning experience for me as well because I believe the day you stop learning is the beginning of your downfall.

'I learnt on a daily basis, from the younger players I played with, how they thought, how they prepared, and shared what I had learnt as well. I remember from my own experience when we were playing against Pakistan, we had 16–17 runs left to win. I had injured my back, and I felt like I was running out of time as I scored boundary after boundary. However, then I got out and we lost 4 wickets soon after. Eventually, we lost the game by 6 or 7 runs. The same thing happened against England in a similar situation. We were chasing 380 runs and Yuvraj and I were batting. He tried a shot.

That's when I told him that ten years ago, it was one of the darkest times, we lost a game we were about to win because of reckless shots. Let's not disrespect the game. Let's continue our partnership, finish it, and let's go smiling back to the dressing room. I shared with Yuvi a lesson I'd learnt ten years ago. All the mistakes we make happen in front of a million people, so we need to train ourselves for that.

'I've left some things for the next generation to follow and if that is my contribution as an Indian cricketer, then I think I have done a decent job. That's how I would like to be known—as someone who inspired the generation after.'

Perhaps the larger message India can learn from cricket and greats like Sachin is his impeccable behaviour on and off the field and the spirit of the Indian dressing room—a melting pot of cultures, religions, backgrounds coming together as Team India for a goal larger than themselves. Their religion: winning for India; their God: Sachin Tendulkar.

Guest Profiles

1. **Pranab Mukherjee:** President of India from 2012–17, he is also a Bharat Ratna. He has previously served as minister of finance, minister of defence, and the minister of external affairs in the UPA government.

2. **Arun Jaitley:** Minister of finance and corporate affairs. He was the minister of information and broadcasting (1999), and minister of law, justice and company affairs (2000) in the Vajpayee government. He was leader of Opposition in the Rajya Sabha during 2009–14. He was also a senior advocate of the Supreme Court.

3. **The Dalai Lama:** At age two, Lhamo Dhondup was identified as the reincarnation of the thirteenth Dalai Lama. He is the spiritual leader of all Tibetan Buddhists. Forced to flee after the Chinese suppression in 1959, he has lived in India ever since. In 1989, he was awarded the Nobel Peace Prize for his non-violent struggle for the liberation of Tibet.

4. **Nirmala Sitharaman:** The current defence minister of India and Rajya Sabha MP from Karnataka.

5. **Amartya Sen:** Indian economist who was awarded the 1998 Nobel Prize in Economic Sciences for his contributions to welfare economics and social choice theory. Awarded the Bharat Ratna in 1999, he is currently a Professor of Economics and Philosophy at Harvard University.

6. **Raghuram Rajan:** He is the Katherine Dusak Miller Distinguished Service Professor of Finance at the Booth School of Business at the University of Chicago. He was the Governor of the Reserve Bank of India during 2013–16. He was the chief economist and director of research at the International Monetary Fund from 2003–2006.

7. **Nandan Nilekani:** Co-founder of tech giant Infosys and its non-executive chairman since August 2017, Nandan Nilekani is credited

215

with building Aadhaar—India's mammoth identity card scheme. He is currently the chairman of a Reserve Bank of India high-level committee to promote digitization of payments.

8. **Aruna Roy:** Indian political and social activist who played a crucial role in the establishment of the Right to Information (RTI) Act and also co-founded the Mazdoor Kisan Shakti Sangathan. She is also a former member of the National Advisory Committee (NAC).

9. **Aamir Khan:** Actor, film-maker and a prominent advocate of social causes, first with a TV show, *Satyamev Jayate*, and now with the Paani Foundation. His work as a social reformer has also earned him a spot in *Time* magazine's list of 100 most influential people in the world.

10. **Kamal Haasan:** Actor in over 200 movies, who has reinvented himself with the launch of his political party, Makkal Needhi Maiam.

11. **Kailash Satyarthi:** An internationally acclaimed child rights activist and humanitarian, Kailash Satyarthi was awarded the Nobel Peace Prize in 2014. He founded the Bachpan Bachao Andolan (Save Childhood Movement) in 1980 to fight for children's rights.

12. **Fali Nariman:** Senior advocate of the Supreme Court and renowned Indian jurist.

13. **Kiran Mazumdar-Shaw:** Chairperson and managing director of Biocon, India's largest biotechnology company, Kiran Mazumdar-Shaw has been ranked in *Forbes* magazine's 'World's 100 Most Powerful Women' list. She recently became a member of the prestigious US National Academy for Engineering.

14. **Sania Mirza:** A former world number one in tennis doubles, Sania Mirza has won six Grand Slam titles. From 2003 until her retirement from singles in 2013, she was ranked by the Women's Tennis Association as India's number one player in both the categories.

15. **Sachin Tendulkar:** Known as the 'God of Cricket', a child prodigy, Tendulkar made his Test debut at the age of sixteen in 1989 against Pakistan. During his twenty-four-year-career, he broke many records including being the first cricketer to play 200 Tests and the first man to score a hundred international hundreds. He is India's youngest Bharat Ratna recipient.